Field Guide to Clandestine Laboratory Identification and Investigation

Clandestine labs that manufacture drugs or explosives may be encountered virtually anywhere. They can range from complex operations employing scientific equipment and exotic chemicals or simply kitchen utensils and chemicals purchased at a local grocery or hardware store. Regardless of their form, the key to detecting clandestine labs is the ability to recognize the combinations of equipment and chemicals that constitute the lab in the first place. The first line of defence against the manufacturers – who supply the drug trade and terrorists with their tools of destruction – is law enforcement, the fire services, and other emergency responders.

Field Guide to Clandestine Laboratory Identification and Investigation, Second Edition provides the information necessary to recognize operations that produce these deadly brews. As with the prior edition, this book has sections covering the chemicals and equipment commonly used in the manufacture of drugs and explosives. They are grouped in a manner that allows the emergency responder to quickly identify common combinations of equipment and chemicals that could potentially be used to manufacture drugs or explosives. Since many clandestine manufacturing operations use commonly available materials that have legitimate uses, the author outlines how to quickly assess and recognize key indicators associated with clandestine laboratory operations.

Sections within the book address information concerning both the hazards associated with those chemicals involved and the personal protective equipment needed to abate the hazards. In addition, documentation requirements, field-testing, and sampling procedures are detailed for use once the operation has been seized and secured. Reproducible worksheets are provided to be used either as, or to supplement, the on-scene investigators' field notes and assist in providing a standardized manner to objectively record information about the crime scene.

The ability to identify the tools used to manufacture contraband drugs and explosives is a key element in the battle against drug abuse and terrorism, making the *Field Guide to Clandestine Laboratory Identification and Investigation, Second Edition* an indispensible resource for responders and investigators alike.

Field Guide to Clandestine Laboratory Identification and Investigation

Second Edition

Donnell R. Christian, Jr.

CRC Press
Taylor & Francis Group
Boca Raton London New York

CRC Press is an imprint of the
Taylor & Francis Group, an **informa** business

Second edition published 2023
by CRC Press
6000 Broken Sound Parkway NW, Suite 300, Boca Raton, FL 33487-2742

and by CRC Press
4 Park Square, Milton Park, Abingdon, Oxon, OX14 4RN

CRC Press is an imprint of Taylor & Francis Group, LLC

First edition published by CRC Press 2004

ISBN: 978-1-032-37062-0 (hbk)
ISBN: 978-1-032-37029-3 (pbk)
ISBN: 978-1-003-33513-9 (ebk)

DOI: 10.4324/9781003335139

Typeset in Minion
by MPS Limited, Dehradun

Contents

Disclaimer to Second Edition

The views expressed in this publication are those of the author and do not necessarily reflect the official policy or position of the Department of Defence or the US government.

Every effort has been made to contact copyright holders for their permission to reprint material in this book. The publishers would be grateful to hear from any copyright holder who is not here acknowledged and will undertake to rectify any errors or omissions in future editions of this book.

About the Author

Donnell R. Christian, Jr. has over 40 years of forensic experience, split between two areas of expertise. He spent 15 years with the Arizona DPS specializing in the clandestine manufacture of drugs and explosives. He is currently an explosives chemist for the Forensic Exploitation Department at the Defense Forensic Science Center. In between these engagements, he assisted in establishing forensic science programs in the developing democracies as the Director of International Training for Professional Business Solutions (PBSI) and as the Forensic Science Development Coordinator for the US DOJ's International Criminal Investigative Training Assistance Program (ICITAP). With ICITAP, he has assisted in establishing forensic science programs in the developing democracies of Armenia, Azerbaijan, Bulgaria, Georgia, Kazakhstan, Kyrgyzstan, Senegal, Turkmenistan, and Uzbekistan as well as the post conflict countries of Bosnia, Haiti, Kosovo, and Iraq. During his tenure with PBSI, he provided the technical assistance to the forensic programs in Armenia, Georgia, and Moldova which lead to their acquisition of ISO 17025 accreditation through their national accreditation body. Mr. Christian has utilized his experience with as the basis for three books and numerous articles to include: *Forensic Investigation of Clandestine Laboratories* (CRC Press 2003), *Field Guide to Clandestine Laboratory Identification and Investigation* (CRC Press 2004), and *Clandestine Lab Investigation Pocket Guide* (PBSI 2006) as well as chapters in *Forensic Science, An Introduction to Forensic Investigative Techniques* (CRC Press 2003, 2005, 2009, 2014) and *The Forensic Science Handbook* (2006, 2011). Donnell has a Bachelor of Science degree in Chemistry and Police Administration from Northern Arizona University and a Masters' Degree in Criminal Justice from AMU.

Preface

Clandestine labs that manufacture drugs and explosives may be observed anywhere. These labs may be located in Skid Row motels or luxury resorts, housing projects or multimillion-dollar homes, and tents in the wilderness or buildings in congested urban areas. They may employ complex scientific equipment and exotic chemicals or simply use kitchen utensils and chemicals purchased at a local grocery or hardware store. Regardless of their form, the key to detection of clandestine labs is the investigator's ability to recognize the combinations of equipment and chemicals that constitute the lab in the first place.

Clandestine drug labs have replaced the moonshiner's still and exchanged it with substances of greater destructive potential. "Super labs" located in rural settings or in jurisdictions just out of the reach of US law enforcement authorities have replaced the large, illegal grain-alcohol distilling operations of prohibition. More critically, bathtub gin has been replaced by stovetop methamphetamine and fentanyl processing operations.

Terrorist activity is not limited to international groups directing their hostility toward a nation. Individuals or small groups can easily hold a city or community hostage through the threatened use of explosives. The common thread among the international terrorists responsible for the first (and possibly second) World Trade Center bombings, the political statements made by disgruntled Americans through the bombing of the Murrah Federal Building in Oklahoma City, and the teenagers who perpetrated the horrors at Columbine High School in Colorado is simply the explosive devices used. In each incident, people employed improvised explosive devices containing clandestinely manufactured explosive mixtures, and in each case the explosive manufacturing was conducted or the devices were constructed in a residential setting.

The front line of defense against the manufacturers who supply the drug trade and terrorist with their tools of destruction is law enforcement, the fire services, and other emergency responders. Their daily contact with the general population under a variety of circumstances provides the opportunity to observe clandestine labs in operation. This *Field Guide to Clandestine Laboratory Identification and Investigation, Second Edition* provides the information necessary to recognize these operations before they can dispense their deadly brews.

This field guide is divided into two basic sections:

1. *The chemicals and equipment commonly used in the manufacture of drugs and explosives.* These are grouped in a manner that allows the emergency responder to quickly identify the combinations of equipment and chemicals that could potentially be used to manufacture drugs or explosives.
2. *The information required to bring order to the chaos of the crime scene.* This segment contains information concerning the hazards associated with the chemicals involved and the personal protective equipment necessary to abate the hazards. Field-testing and sampling procedures are delineated for use once the operation has been seized and secured. Finally, reproducible worksheets that can be used for working notes or to supplement the on-scene investigators' field notes are provided. The object here is to record as much information as possible about the crime scene in a standardized manner, thus minimizing later judicial loss through inadvertent technicalities.

The ability to identify the tools used to manufacture deadly brews of drugs and explosives is a key element in the battle against drug abuse and terrorism. Unfortunately, many of the clandestine manufacturing operations use materials that have legitimate uses and are commonly available. The *Field Guide to Clandestine Laboratory Identification and Investigation, Second Edition* provides its users the ability to identify combinations of commonly encountered chemicals and equipment that can potentially produce drugs and explosives and to address a manufacturing operation if one is suspected. Use it in good health.

Donnell R. Christian, Jr.

Definitions

1

Catalyst	A chemical that is used to initiate a chemical reaction.
Clandestine Lab	An illicit operation consisting of a sufficient combination of apparatus and chemicals that either has been or could be used in the manufacture or synthesis of controlled substances.
Controlled substance	Any compound that the possession and distribution of which is controlled by the government. This term is generally applied to drugs. However, the sale and distribution of explosives is also controlled by the government.
Conversion	The process of changing a drug or chemical from one form to another. For example, converting a cocaine hydrochloride to free base cocaine (crack). Conversion can also include slightly modifying the chemical structure of the precursor chemical to convert it into the final product. For example, converting pseudoephedrine into methamphetamine.
Distillation	The process of separating components in a mixture by using the differences in their boiling. Individual components evaporate from the mixture, are condensed and collected in a separate container.
Drug	The Federal Food, Drug, and Cosmetic Act definition of "drug" includes "articles intended for use in the diagnosis, cure, mitigation, treatment, or prevention of disease in man or other animals" and "articles (other than food) intended to affect the structure or any function of the body of man or other animals."
Explosive	Chemicals that undergo a rapid chemical change that releases large amounts of heat and gas.
Extraction	The process of separating a chemical component from the bulk mixture. For example, extracting pseudoephedrine from pharmaceutical tablets or extracting methamphetamine from a reaction mixture. No structural changes occur to the target molecule.
Hydrogenation	A chemical reaction that replaces part of a molecule with a hydrogen atom. This reaction is conducted under high pressure in the presence of hydrogen and a catalyst.
Reflux	Using a controlled boil to conduct a chemical synthesis. The vapors from the boiling chemical reaction are condensed and returned to the reaction mixture.
Solvent	A chemical used to facilitate a chemical reaction or a liquid extraction. Solvents do not react directly with reagent or precursor chemicals.
Synthesis	The process of combining precursor chemicals into a new compound. The chemical structure of the final product is a combination of the chemical structures of the precursors involved.
Tableting	The process of preparing bulk drugs for sale distribution of individual use.

DOI: 10.4324/9781003335139-1

Equipment

2

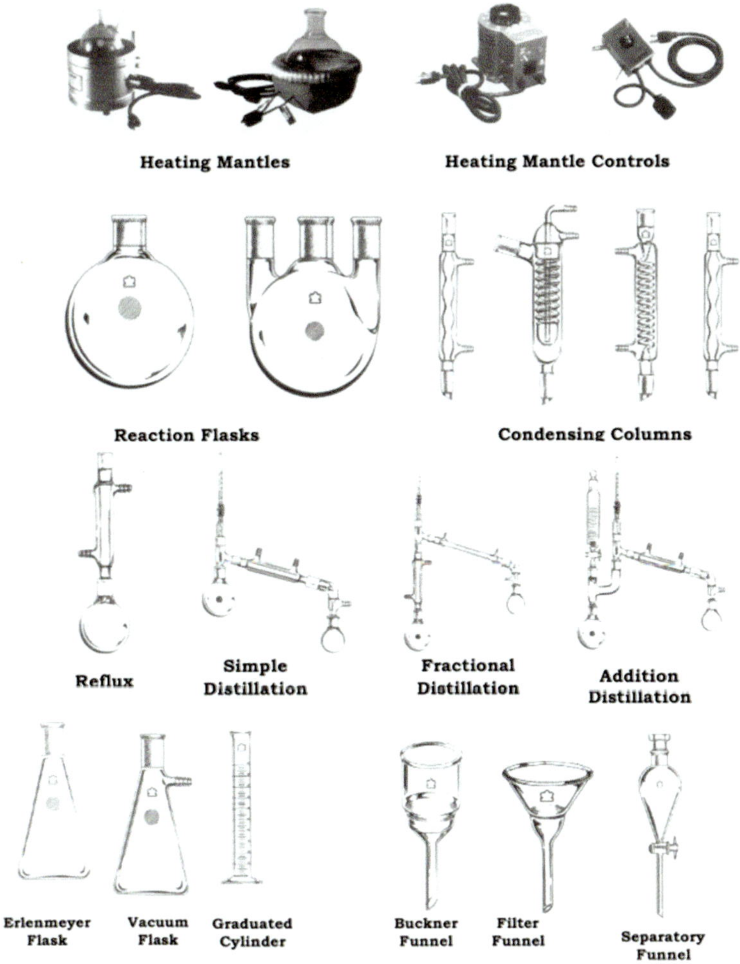

Figure 2.1 Traditional Scientific Equipment.

DOI: 10.4324/9781003335139-2

Clandestine Operations

Figure 2.2 Reflux Apparatus.

Figure 2.3 Distillation Apparatus.

Figure 2.4 Hydrogenation Apparatus.

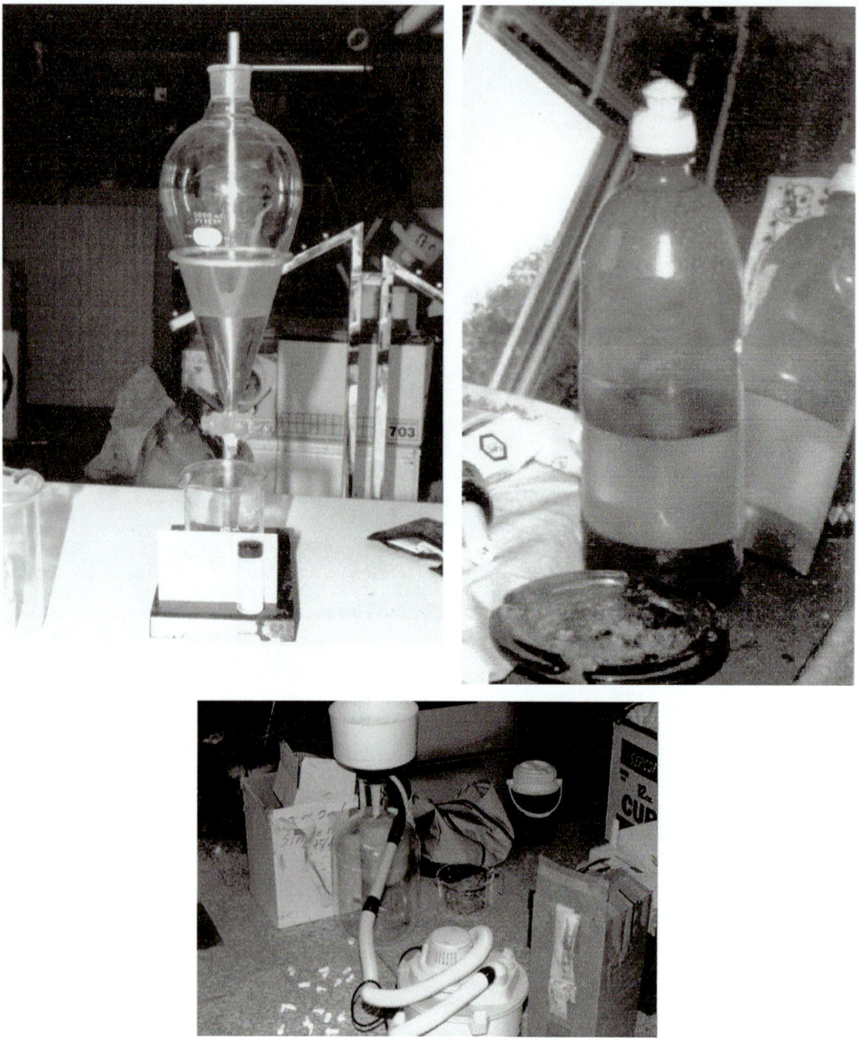

Figure 2.5 Extraction Apparatus.

Figure 2.6 Hydrogen Iodide Generator.

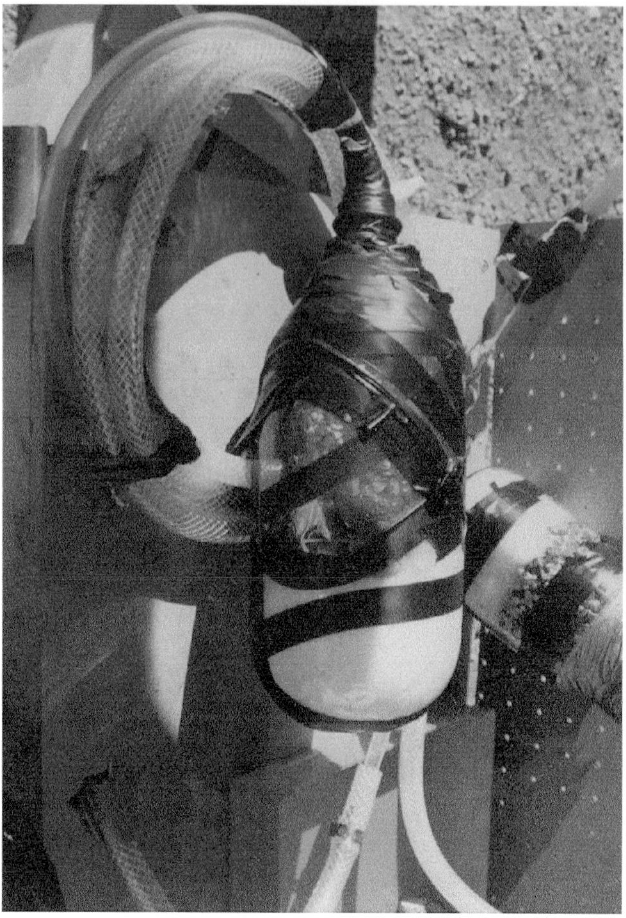

Figure 2.7 Fume Filtration Apparatus.

Figure 2.8 Hydrogen Chloride Generator.

Clandestine Manufacturing Equipment

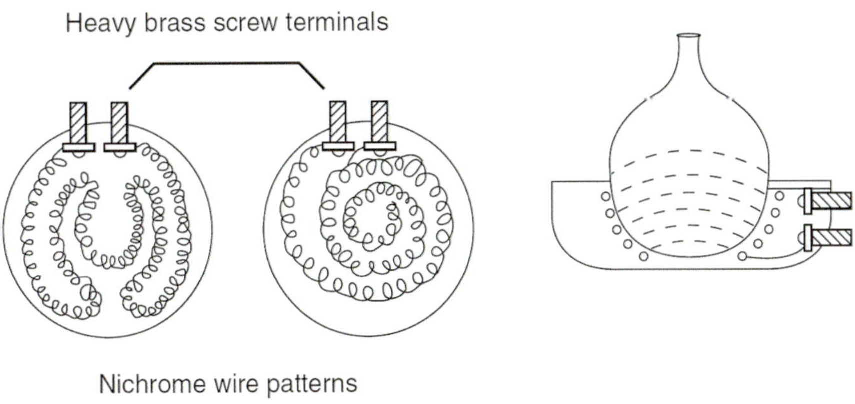

Figure 2.9 Heating Mantle (from *The Whole Drug Manufactures Catalogue*, Chewbacca Darth, Shmootz & Goniff Publishing, Co. 1980. With permission).

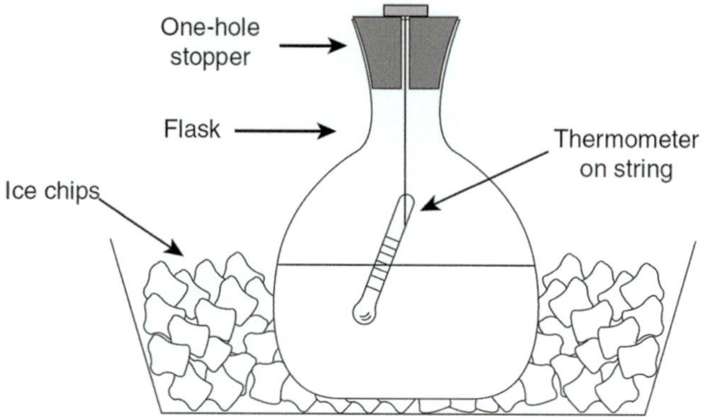

Figure 2.10 Ice Bath (from *The Whole Drug Manufactures Catalogue*, Chewbacca Darth, Shmootz & Goniff Publishing, Co. 1980. With permission).

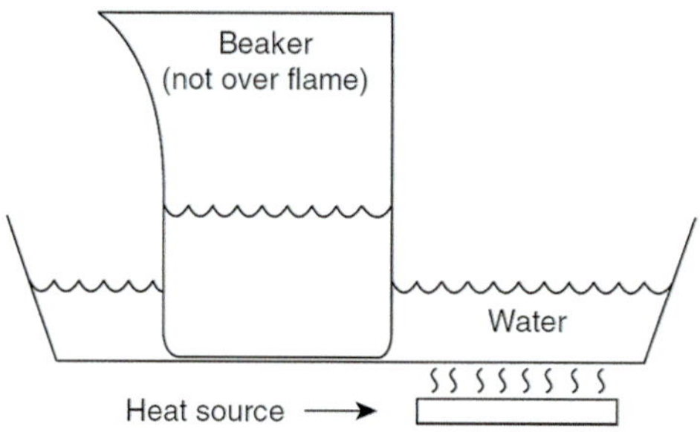

Figure 2.11 Water Bath (from *The Whole Drug Manufactures Catalogue*, Chewbacca Darth, Shmootz & Goniff Publishing, Co. 1980. With permission).

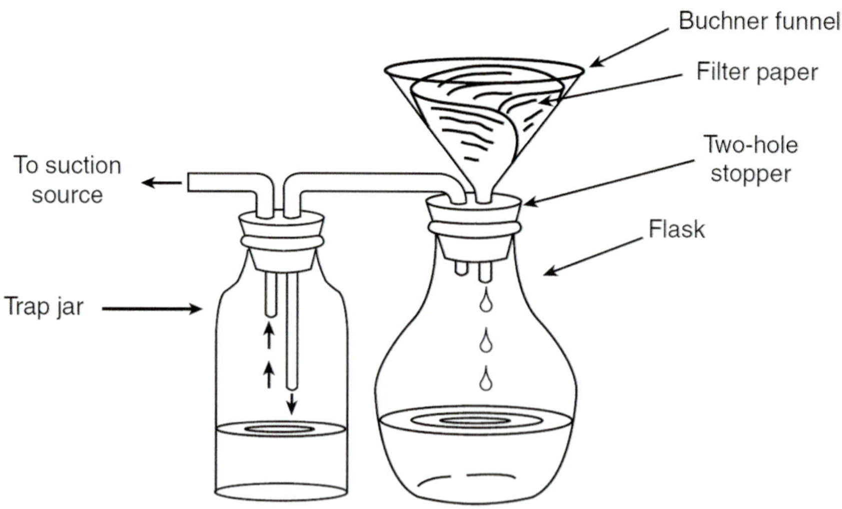

Figure 2.12 Vacuum Filtration (from *The Whole Drug Manufactures Catalogue*, Chewbacca Darth, Shmootz & Goniff Publishing, Co. 1980. With permission).

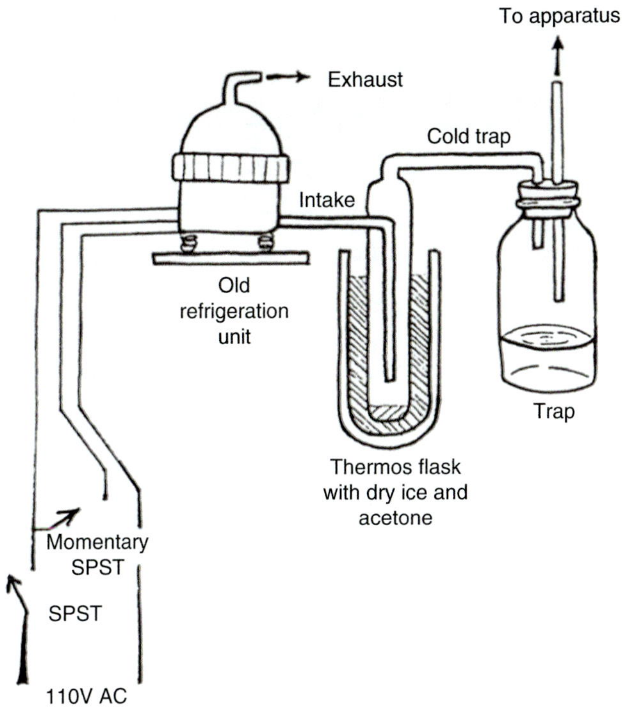

Figure 2.13 Vacuum Pump (from *The Whole Drug Manufactures Catalogue*, Chewbacca Darth, Shmootz & Goniff Publishing, Co. 1980. With permission).

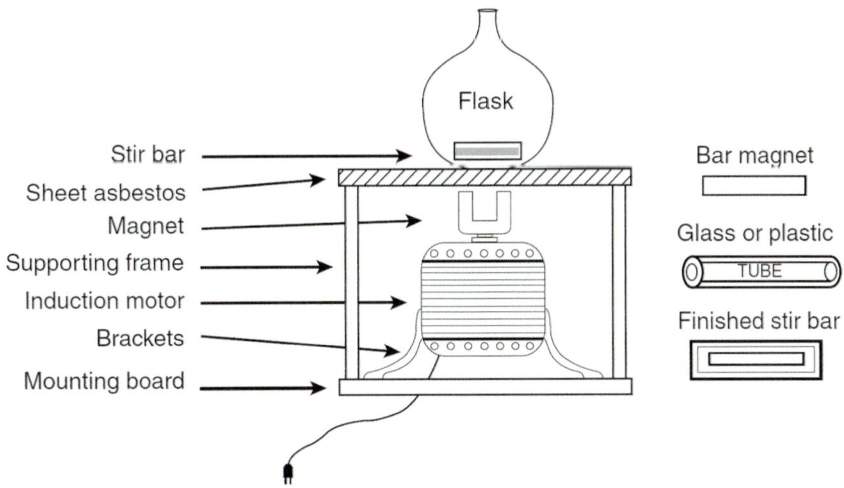

Figure 2.14 Magnetic Stirrer (from *The Whole Drug Manufactures Catalogue*, Chewbacca Darth, Shmootz & Goniff Publishing, Co. 1980. With permission).

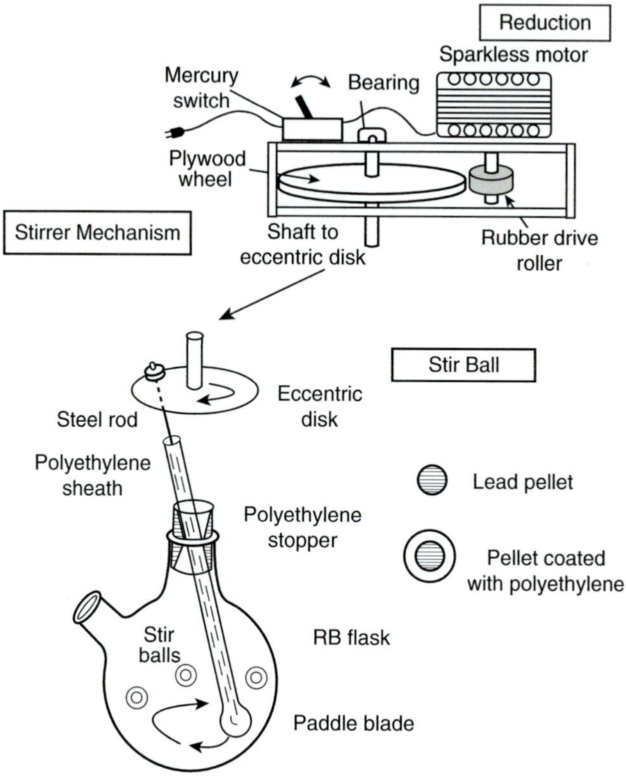

Figure 2.15 Mechanical Stirrer (from *The Whole Drug Manufactures Catalogue*, Chewbacca Darth, Shmootz & Goniff Publishing, Co. 1980. With permission).

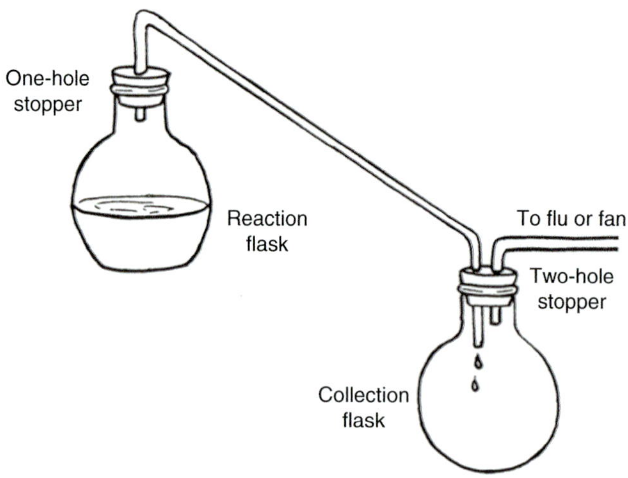

Figure 2.16 Aspirator (from *The Whole Drug Manufactures Catalogue*, Chewbacca Darth, Shmootz & Goniff Publishing, Co. 1980. With permission).

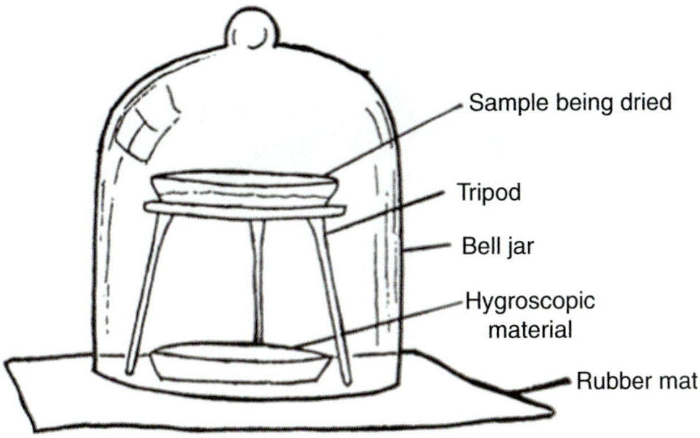

Figure 2.17 Desiccator (from *The Whole Drug Manufactures Catalogue*, Chewbacca Darth, Shmootz & Goniff Publishing, Co. 1980. With permission).

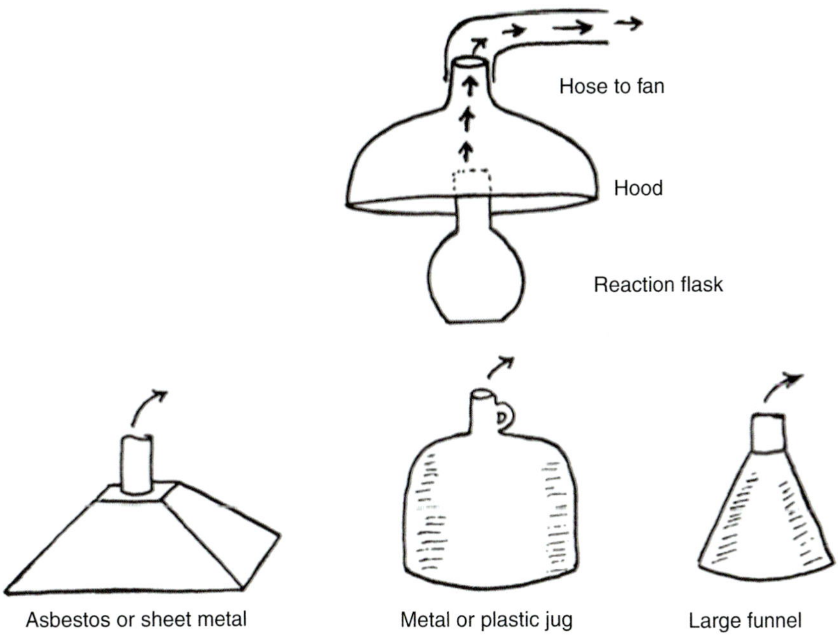

Figure 2.18 Fume Hood Variations (from *The Whole Drug Manufactures Catalogue*, Chewbacca Darth, Shmootz & Goniff Publishing, Co. 1980. With permission).

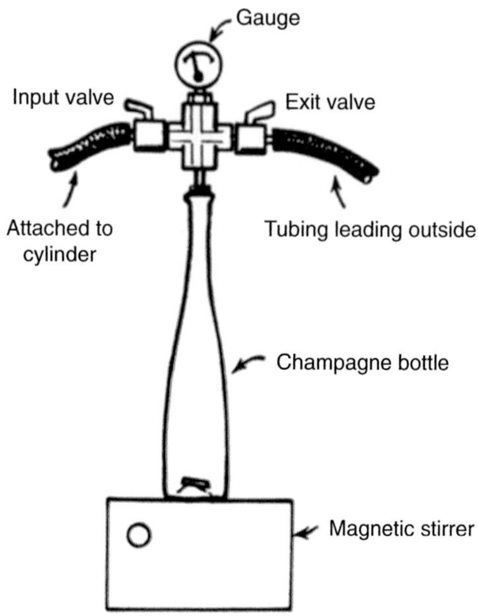

Figure 2.19 Hydrogenator (from *The Secrets of Methamphetamine, Fifth Edition,* Uncle Fester, Loompanics Unlimited. 1999. With permission).

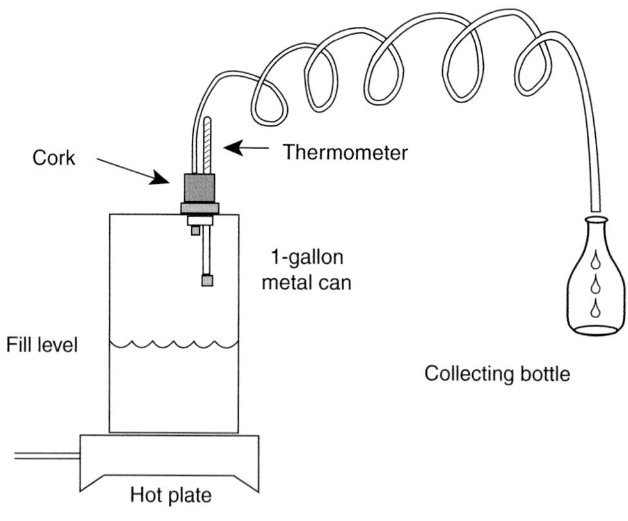

Figure 2.20 Coiled Metal Tube Still (from *Home Workshop Explosives,* Uncle Fester, Festering Publications, 826 S. Baird, Green Bay, WI 54301. With permission).

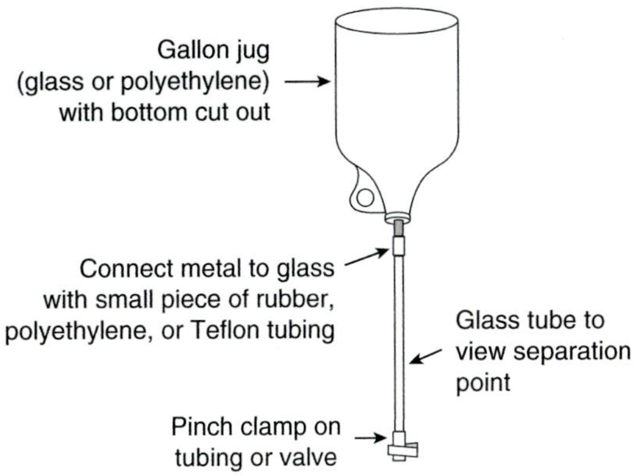

Figure 2.21 Homemade Separatory Funnell (from *The Construction and Operation of Clandestine Drug Laboratories, Second Edition*, Jack B. Nimble, Loompanics Unlimited. PO Box 1197, Port Townsend, WA 98369. With permission).

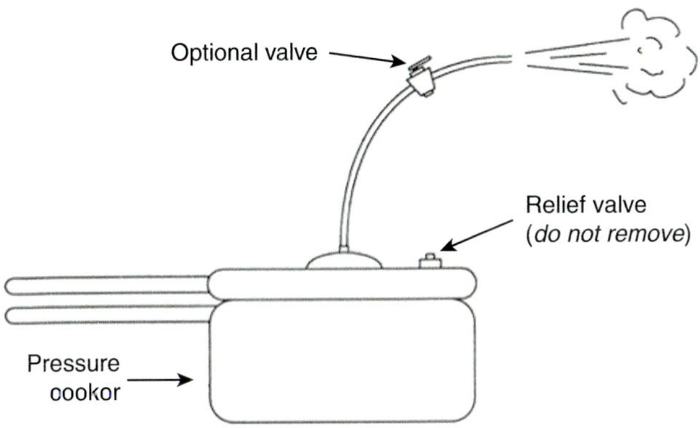

Figure 2.22 Pressure Cooker Reaction Vessel (from *The Construction and Operation of Clandestine Drug Laboratories, Second Edition*, Jack B. Nimble, Loompanics Unlimited. PO Box 1197, Port Townsend, WA 98369. With permission).

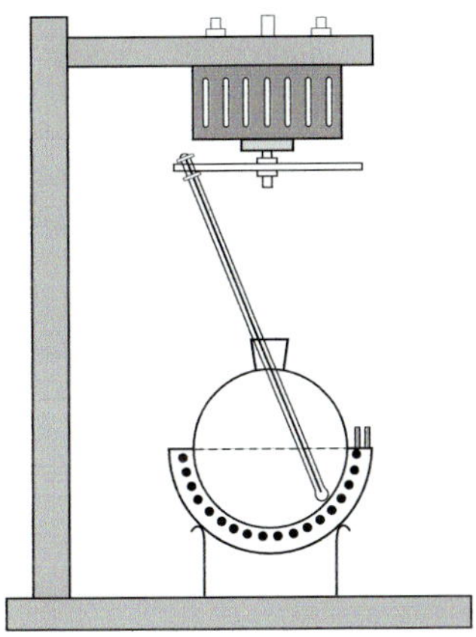

Figure 2.23 Mechanical Stirrer (from *The Construction and Operation of Clandestine Drug Laboratories, Second Edition*, Jack B. Nimble, Loompanics Unlimited. PO Box 1197, Port Townsend, WA 98369. With permission).

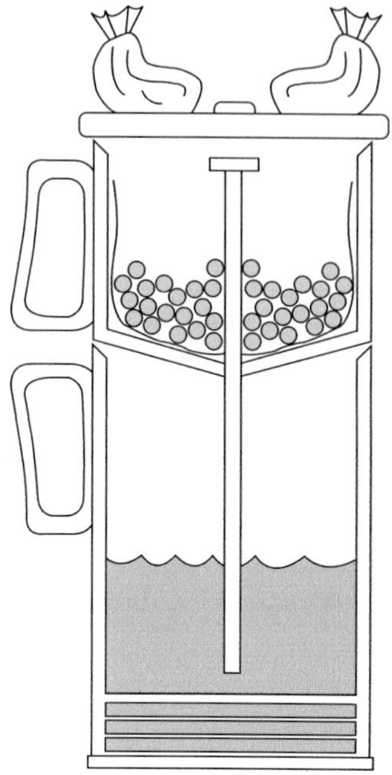

Figure 2.24 Reflux Extraction A (from *The Construction and Operation of Clandestine Drug Laboratories, Second Edition*, Jack B. Nimble, Loompanics Unlimited. PO Box 1197, Port Townsend, WA 98369. With permission).

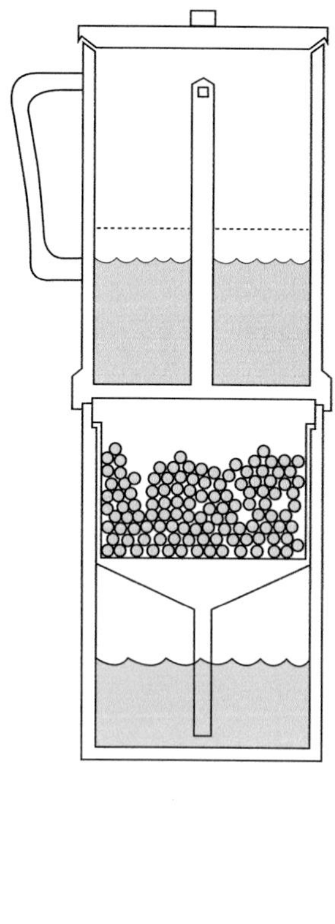

Figure 2.25 Reflux Extraction B (from *The Construction and Operation of Clandestine Drug Laboratories, Second Edition*, Jack B. Nimble, Loompanics Unlimited. PO Box 1197, Port Townsend, WA 98369. With permission).

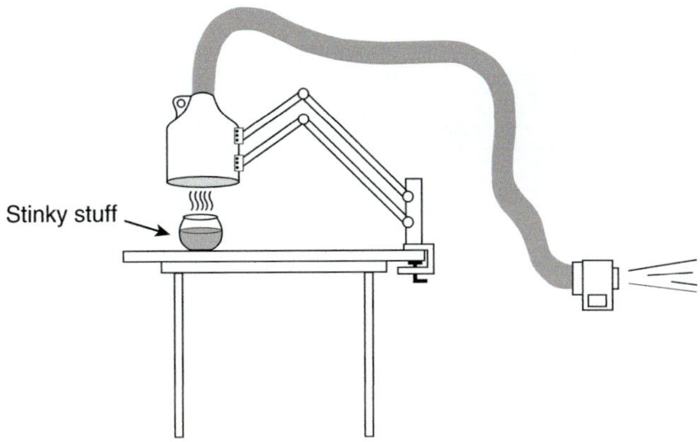

Figure 2.26 Fume Hood (from *The Construction and Operation of Clandestine Drug Laboratories, Second Edition*, Jack B. Nimble, Loompanics Unlimited. PO Box 1197, Port Townsend, WA 98369. With permission).

IED Components

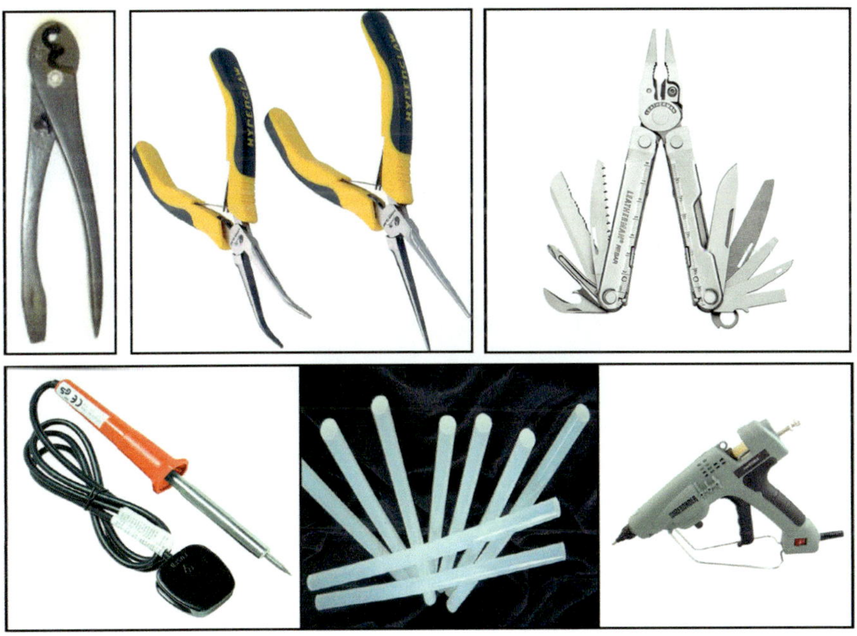

Figure 2.27 Bomber Tools.

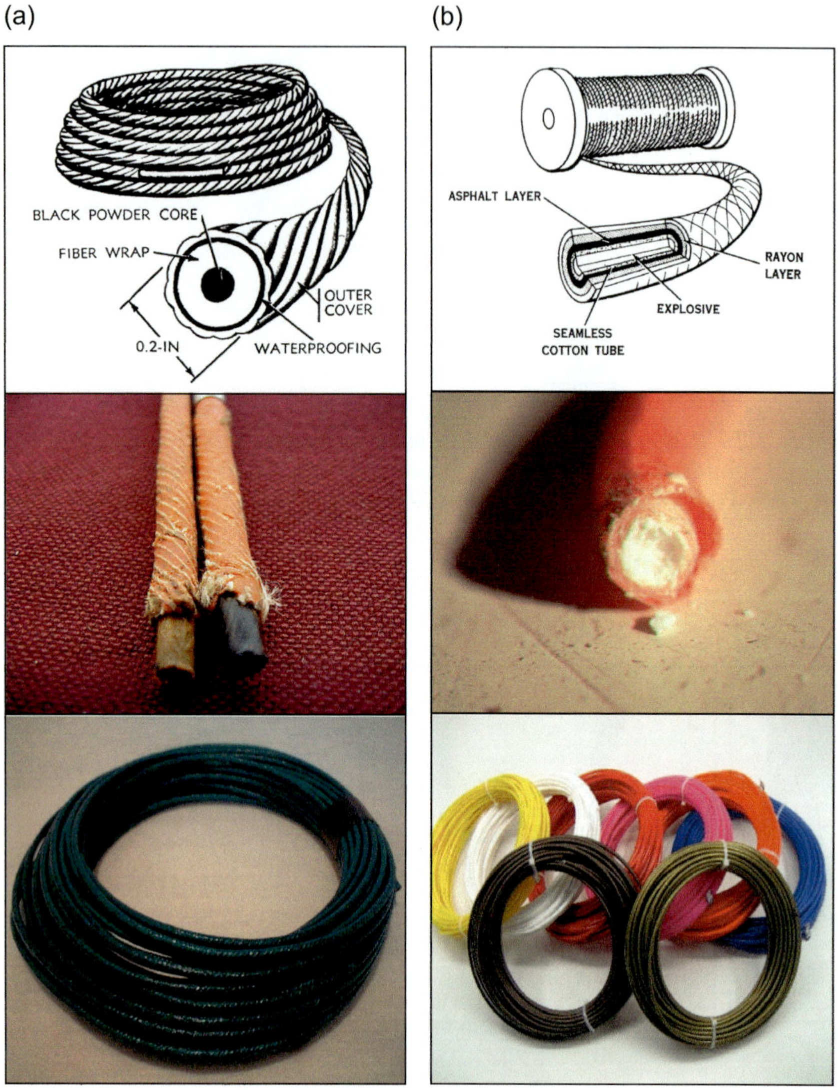

Figure 2.28 (a) Safety Fuse, (b) Detonation Cord.

Figure 2.29 (a) Black Powder, (b) Pyrodex (c) Smokeless Powder.

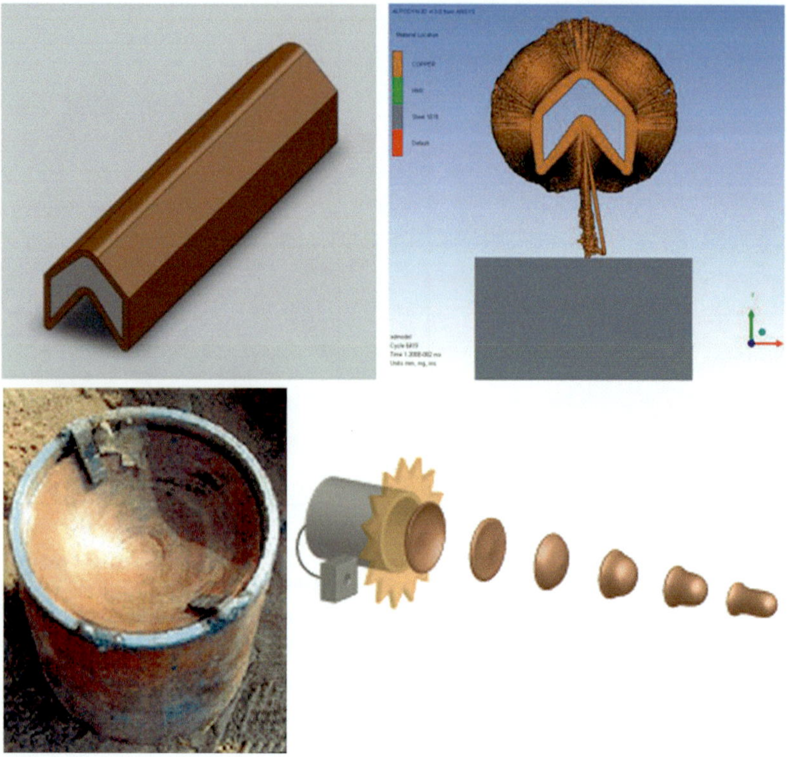

Figure 2.30 Shaped Charges.

Figure 2.31 Ammonium Nitrate.

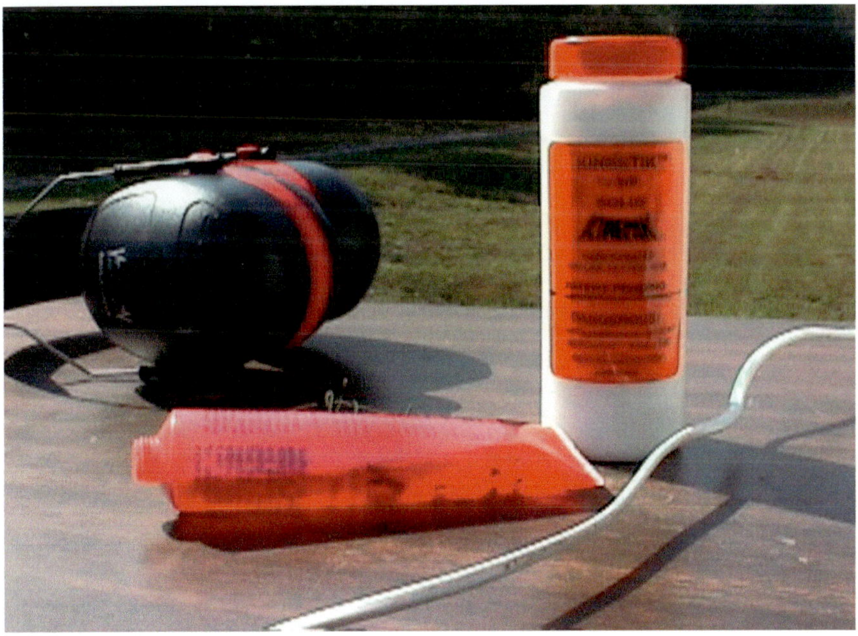

Figure 2.32 Binary Explosive.

Figure 2.33 Non-Electric Blasting Cap.

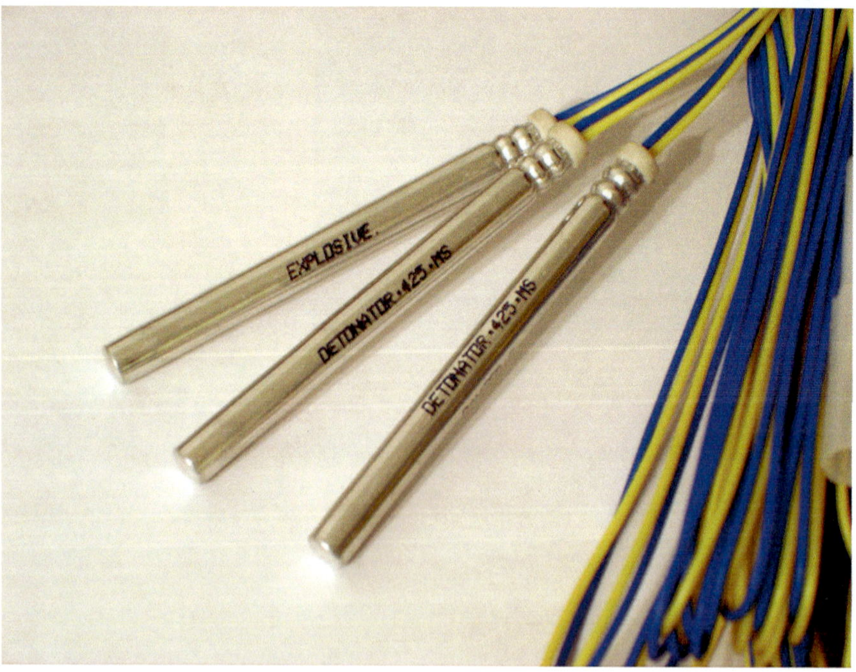

Figure 2.34 Electric Blasting Cap.

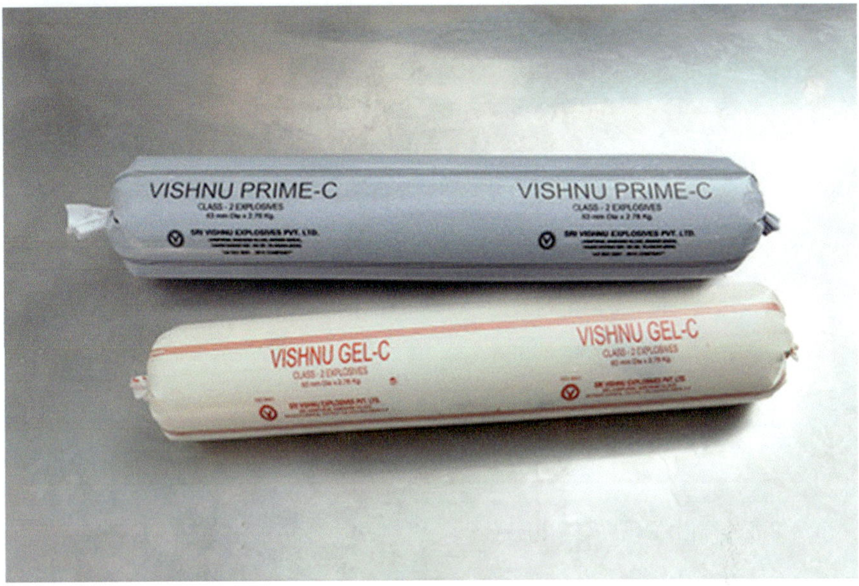

Figure 2.35 Gelatin/Slurry Dynamite.

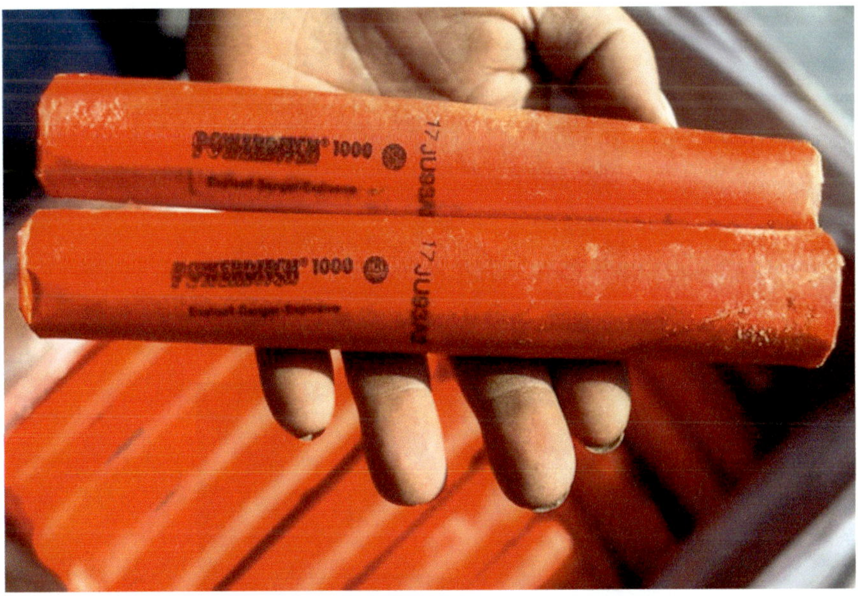

Figure 2.36 Traditional Dynamite.

Figure 2.37 Military TNT Blocks.

Figure 2.38 Blasting Machines.

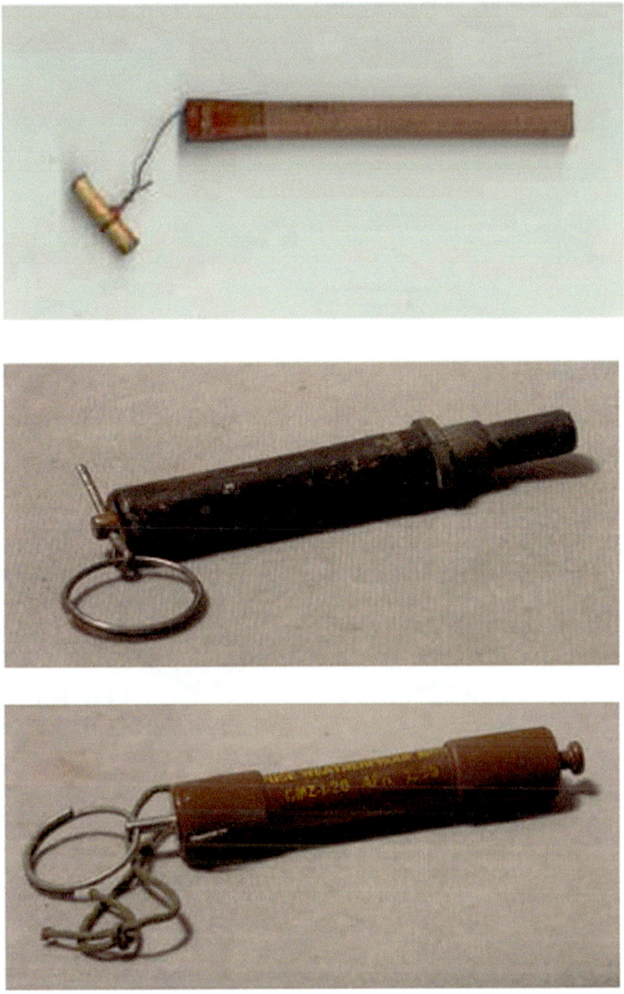

Figure 2.39 Fuse Igniters.

Figure 2.40 Grenades.

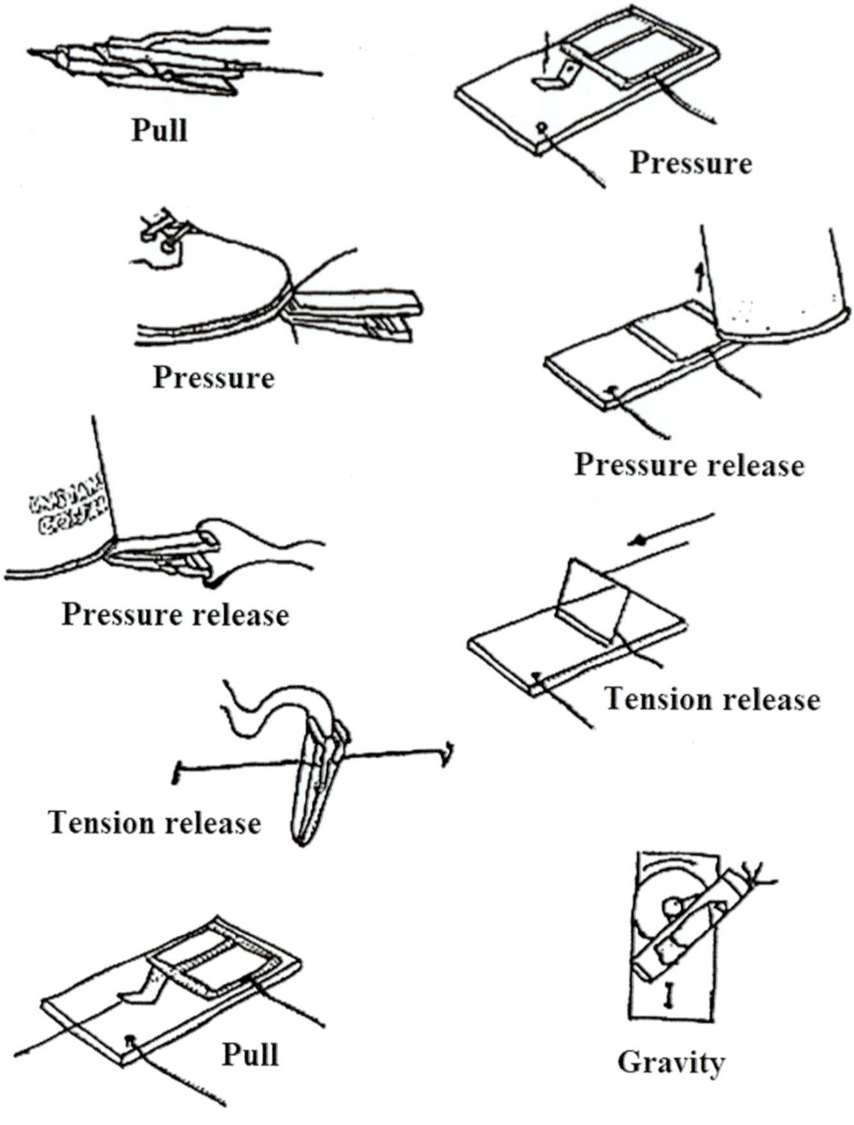

Figure 2.41 Improvised Switches.

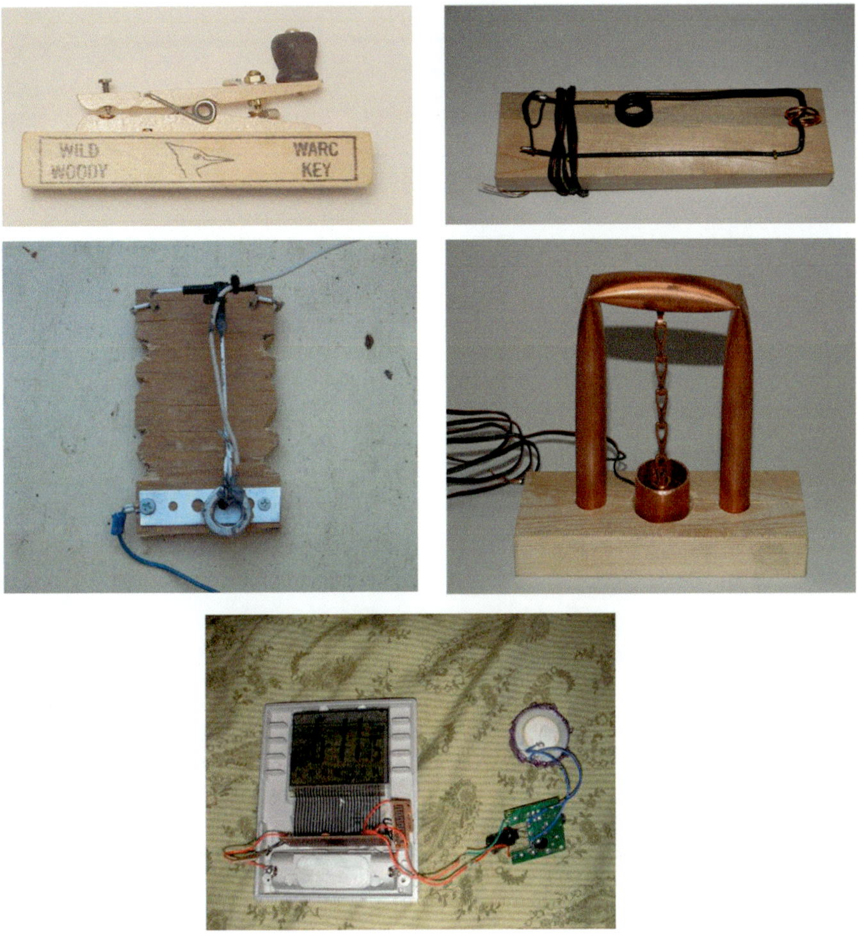

Figure 2.42 Improvised Switches.

Figure 2.43 Electric Match.

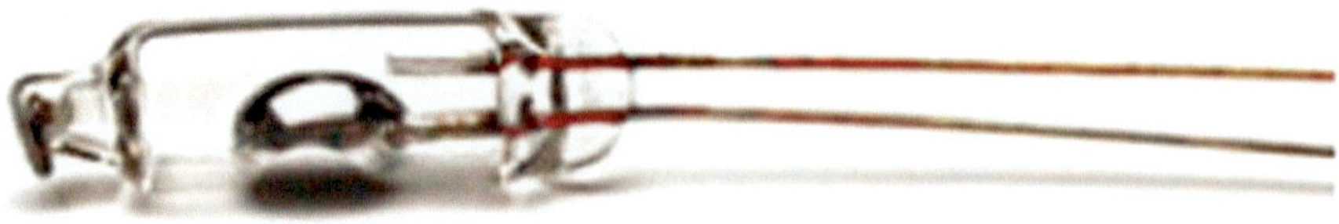

Figure 2.44 Mercury Switch.

Figure 2.45 (a–c) Improvised Explosive Devices (IEDs).

Chemical Tables

3

Table 3.1 Legitimate Uses

Chemical	Legitimate Uses
Acetaldehyde*	Manufacture of perfumes, flavors, plastics; silver mirrors
Acetic Acid*	Food preservative; organic synthesis
Acetic Anhydride*	Organic synthesis; dehydrating agent
Acetone	General solvent
Acetonitrile*	Solvent; organic synthesis
Allylbenzene*	None Listed
Allylchloride*	Organic synthesis
4 Allyl 1,2 Methylenedioxybenzene*	None Listed
Aluminum Powder	Paint additive, pyrotechnics, explosives, metal alloys
Aluminum Chloride*	Disinfectant, deodorant, wood preservative
Ammonia Gas*	Refrigerant; manufacture of nitric acid, fertilizer, explosives
Ammonium Chloride*	Batteries, electroplating, textiles
Ammonium Formate*	Inorganic metal analysis
Ammonium Hydroxide*	None Listed
Ammonium Nitrate	Fertilizer, explosives, matches, pyrotechnics
Aniline*	Manufacture of dyes, perfumes, varnishes, organic synthesis
Aspirine	Over the counter medicine
Benzaldehyde*	Manufacture of dyes, perfumes, flavors
Barium Chlorate	Pyrotechnics, explosives, matches, dye processes
Barium Nitrate	Pyrotechnics, explosives, vacuum tube manufacture
Benzene*	Manufacture of pharmaceuticals, dyes; industrial solvent

(Continued)

DOI: 10.4324/9781003335139-3

Table 3.1 (Continued) Legitimate Uses

Chemical	Legitimate Uses
Benzyl Chloride*	Manufacture of dyes, pharmaceutical, perfumes, resins
Benzyl Cyanide*	None Listed
Bromobenzene*	Manufacture of Grignard reagent
Bromoethane*	None Listed
Carbon Dioxide	Beverage carbonation, fire extinguisher, dry ice
Carbon Tetrachoride*	Dry cleaning, fire extinguisher, general solvent
Chloro-2-Propanone*	Intermediate for perfumes, drugs, insecticides: photography
Copper Oxide	Ceramic and glass pigment, glass polishing
Copper Sulfate	Fungicide, photography, food additive, paint pigment
Cyclohexanone*	Industrial solvent
Dichloroethane*	None Listed
Ephedrine*	Bronchodialator
Ergotamine Tartrate*	Treatment of migraine headaches
Eythritol	Sugar substitute
Ethyl Acetate*	Manufacture of photo film, perfume, gun powder, dry cleaning
Etylene Glycol	Antifreeze, polymer precursor
Formamide*	Organic synthesis
Formic Acid*	Tanning, electroplating, wool dying
Glygerin	Food preservative, antimicrobial, soap production
Guanidine	Plastic production
Hexamine	Heating tablets
Hydrazine	Reducing agent, rocket fuel
Hydrobromic Acid*	Analytical reagent
Hydrochloric Acid	Pool chemical, masonry and metal cleaner, mining
Hydrogen	Welding
Hydrogen Peroxide*	Rocket fuel, bleaching agent
Hydriodic Acid*	Manufacture of pharmaceutical, disinfectants
Hydroxylamine HCL*	Photography, antioxidant for soaps
Iodine*	Manufacture of germicides and antiseptics; catalyst
Lithium Metal*	Catalyst, metal alloys, batteries
Lithium Aluminum Hydride*	Reducing agent
Lithium Hydroxide	Photographic developers
Magnesium Metal	Metal alloys, pyrotechnics, Grignard reagent

Table 3.1 (Continued) Legitimate Uses

Chemical	Legitimate Uses
Mannitol	Sweetener, food additive, pharmaceutical applications
Mercuric Chloride	Preservative; photography, mining, steel etching
Mercury*	Thermometers, switches, lighting, mining, dentistry
Methanol	Solvent, antifreeze, gas additive, camping fuel
Methyl Acrylate*	Manufacture of plastics and textiles
Methylamine*	Tanning; organic synthesis
Methyl Ethyl Ketone	Industrial solvent, auto painting
Nitric Acid	Manufacture of fertilizers, dyes, explosives and a variety of organic chemicals
Nitroethane	Fuel additive, solvent
Perchloric Acid*	Metal plating; explosives
Peroxide	Disinfectant, hair coloring, organic synthesis
Pentaerythrotol	Fire retardant, paints and coating, organic synthesis
Phenylacetic Acid*	Manufacture of perfumes
Phenylacetonitrile*	Organic synthesis
Phenylmagnesium Bromide*	Organic synthesis
Phosphoric Acid*	Manufacture of fertilizers, detergents; food additive; cleaning solvent
Phosphorous Red*	Pyrotechnics; matches; fertilizers; pesticides
Phosphorous Pentachloride*	Catalyst
Piperidine*	Organic synthesis
Potassium Carbonate	Manufacture of soap, glass, pottery; engraving; tanning
Potassium Chlorate	Explosives, pyrotechnics, matches, dye industry
Potassium Chromate	Leather tanning, rust proofing metal
Potassium Cyanide	Mining, electroplating, steel hardening
Potassium Dichromate	Leather tanning, dyes, paints, pyrotechnics, matches, waterproofing fabrics
Potassium Hydroxide	Paint/varnish remover, photo engraving, printing inks
Potassium Iodide	Oxidizer for chemical analysis
Potassium Nitrate	Tempering steel, tobacco curing, glass manufacture, explosives
Potassium Perchlorate	Explosives, pyrotechnics, photography
Propylene Glycol	Food additive, anti-freeze, polymer production
Pyridine*	Solvent, organic synthesis
Rainey Nickel*	Catalyst

(*Continued*)

Table 3.1 (Continued) Legitimate Uses

Chemical	Legitimate Uses
Sodium Metal*	Manufacture of sodium compounds, sodium vapor lamps
Sodium Acetate	Photography, food additive
Sodium Bicarbonate	Baking soda, fire extinguishers, cleaning compounds
Sodium Bisulfite	Disinfectant; textile bleaching; food additive
Sodium Hydroxide	Drain cleaner
Sodium Nitrate*	Glass manufacturing, pottery, fertilizer, meat and tobacco preparation
Strontium Nitrate	Pyrotechnics, road flares, matches
Sulfur	Vulcanization of black rubber, fertilizer, fungicide and production of sulfuric acid
Sulfuric Acid	Battery acid; drain cleaner; manufacture of fertilizers, explosives
Tartaric Acid	Food additive; photography; tanning; ceramics
Thorium Nitrate*	Catalyst
Toluene	Paint solvent, industrial chemical, printing and leather tanning processes
Trifluro Acetic Anhydride*	None listed
Urea	Fertilizers, pharmaceutical applications
Zinc Metal	Metal alloys, batteries, mining, printing plates, household utensils

* No legitimate home or hobby use.

Table 3.2 Clandestine Use Table (Drugs)

	Amphetamine	Cocaine	Heroin	MDA/MDMA	Methamphetamine	PCP analogs	P-2-P
Acetic Acid	*		*	*			*
Acetic Anhydride			*				*
Acetaldehyde					*		
Acetonitrile	*						
a-Acetylphenylacetonitrile							*
Allyl Benzene	*				*		
Allyl Chloride	*				*		
4-Allyl-1,2-Methylenedioxy Benzene				*			
Aluminum Foil	*				*		
Aluminum Chloride				*			*
Ammonia Gas	*		*	*	*		
Ammonium Acetate	*			*			
Ammonium Chloride			*		*		
Ammonium Formate	*			*		*	
Ammonium Hydroxide	*					*	
Benzaldehyde	*						*
Benzene	*						*
Benzyl Chloride					*		
Benzyl Cyanide							*
Bromobenzene						*	
Bromothiophene						*	

(Continued)

Table 3.2 (Continued) Clandestine Use Table (Drugs)

	Amphetamine	Cocaine	Heroin	MDA/MDMA	Methamphetamine	PCP analogs	P-2-P
Butylamine	*						
Calcium Oxide (anhydrous lime)		*	*				
Chloroacetone							*
3-Chloropropene	*				*		
Copper Sulfate					*		
Cuprus Oxide				*			
Cyclohexanone						*	
Dibromomethane				*			
Ephedrine/Psuedoephedrine					*		
Ethyl Acetate							*
Formamide	*			*			
Formic Acid	*			*	*		
Hydrobromic Acid (HBr)				*			
Hydrochloric Acid (HCl)	*	*	*	*	*	*	
Hydrogen	*				*		
Hydrogen Peroxide				*			
Hydroidic Acid (HI0)	*				*		
Hydroxylamine HCl	*						
Iodine					*		
Iron Fillings							*
Isosafrole				*			
Lithium					*		
Lithium Aluminum Hydride	*			*			

Table 3.2 (Continued) Clandestine Use Table (Drugs)

	Amphetamine	Cocaine	Heroin	MDA/MDMA	Methamphetamine	PCP analogs	P-2-P
Magnesium Turnings					*	*	
Manganous Carbonate							*
Manganous Chloride							*
Mercuric Chloride	*			*	*		
Mercury	*						
Methylamine				*	*		*
Methylformamide				*	*		*
Nitroethane				*			*
Norpseudoephedrine	*						
Palladium Sulfate					*		
Perchloric Acid					*		
Phenylacetic Acid							*
Phenylacetontrile							*
Phenylmagnesium Bromide						*	
Phenylacetone	*				*		
Phosphorous	*				*		
Phosphorous Pentachloride					*		
Piperidine						*	
Piperonal				*			
Platinum					*		
Platinum Chloride					*		
Platinum Oxide					*		
Potassium Carbonate						*	

(Continued)

Table 3.2 (Continued) Clandestine Use Table (Drugs)

	Amphetamine	Cocaine	Heroin	MDA/MDMA	Methamphetamine	PCP analogs	P-2-P
Potassium Cyanide						*	
Potassium Hydroxide	*			*	*	*	*
Pumic							*
Pyridine						*	
Raney Nickle	*				*		
Sodium					*		
Sodium Acetate							*
Sodium Amalgum	*						
Sodium Bisulfite						*	*
Sodium Carbonate			*				
Sodium Hydroxide	*	*		*	*	*	*
Sodium Sulfate	*						*
Sulfuric Acid	*	*		*	*		*
Thionyl Chloride					*		

Manufacturing Method Tables (Drugs)

Table 3.3 Amphetamine

Amphetamine	Precursors	Reagents
A1: Amphetamine via Leuckart reaction	Ammonia Ammonium formate Formamide Phenylacetone	Formic acid Hydrochloric acid Sulfuric acid
A2: Amphetamine via benzaldehyde/nitroethane	Benzaldehyde Nitroethane	Acetic acid Butylamine Hydrogen Lithium aluminum hydride Sodium amalgum Raney nickel
A3: Amphetamine via P-2-P/ hydroxylamine	Hydroxylamine HCl Phenylacetone	Acetic acid Hydrogen Lithium aluminum hydride Raney nickel Palladium black Sodium acetate Sodium amalgum
A4: Amphetamine via P-2-P/ ammonia	Ammonia Phenylacetone	Aluminum Mercuric chloride
A5: Amphetamine via benzene/ allyl chloride/ammonia	Benzene Allyl chloride Ammonia	Ferric chloride
A6: Amphetamine via allylbenzene/acetonitrile	Allybenzene Acetonitrile	Hydrochloric acid
A7: Amphetamine via phenylpropanolamine/HI	Phenylpropanolamine	Hydriodic acid Red phosphorous

Table 3.4 MDA/MDMA

MDA/MDMA	Precursors	Reagents
MD1: MDA via Isosafrole to 3,4-methylenedioxy P-2-P using the leuckart reaction	Ammonia Ammonium formate Formamide Isosafrole	Acetic acid Formic acid Hydrochloric acid Hydrogen peroxide Sulfuric acid

(Continued)

Table 3.4 (Continued) MDA/MDMA

MDA/MDMA	Precursors	Reagents
MD2: MDA via piperonal/ nitroethane	Nitroethane Piperonal	Acetic acid Ammonium acetate Lithium aluminum hydride
MD3: MDMA via 3,4-methylenedioxy P-2-P/ methylamine	Isosafrole Methylamine	Aluminum foil Mercuric chloride
MD4: MDMA via 3,4-methylenedioxy P-2-P using the Leuckart reaction	Isosafrole Methylamine Methylformamide	Acetic acid Formic acid Hydrochloric acid Hydrogen peroxide Sulfuric acid
MD5a: MDA via safrole/HBr/ ammonia **MD5b:** MDMA via safrole/HBr/ methylamine	Ammonia (MDA) Methylamine (MDMA) Safrole	Cuprus oxide Hydrobromic acid Mercuric chloride Sodium carbonate Sodium hydroxide

Table 3.5 Methamphetamine

Methamphetamine	Precursors	Reagents
M1: Methamphetamine via P-2-P/methylamine	Phenylacetone Methylamine	Aluminum Mercuric chloride
M2: Methamphetamine via ephedrine/H_2	Ephedrine	Hydrogen Palladium black Palladium sulfate Perchloric acid Phosphorous pentachloride Platinum Platinum chloride Sodium acetate Sulfuric acid Thionyl chloride
M3: Mehtamphetamine via ephedrine/HI	Ephedrine	Hydriodic acid Iodine Red phosphorous
M4: Methamphetamine via benzyl chloride/acetaldehyde/ methylamine	Acetaldehyde Benzylchloride Methylamine	Iodine Magnesium
M5: Methamphetamine via Leuckart reaction	Phenylacetone Methylamine Methylformamide	Formic acid Hydrochloric acid

Table 3.5 (Continued) Methamphetamine

Methamphetamine	Precursors	Reagents
M6: Methamphetamine via benzene/allyl chloride/ methylamine	Allyl chloride Benzene Methylamine	Ferric chloride
M7: Methamphetamine via Birch reduction (Nazi method)	Ephedrine	Ammonia Ammonium chloride Lithium or sodium Sodium chloride Tetrahydrofuran

Table 3.6 Fentanyl Manufacturing

Fentanyl Analogs	Precursors	Reagents
Fentanyl/Acetylfentanyl	4-Piperidone monohydrate hydrochloride (2-bromoethyl) benzene Aniline Diisopropylethylamine (DIPEA) Acetic anhydride	Acetic acid Cesium carbonate (CsCO) Sodium triacetoxyborohydride Propionyl chloride Hydrochloric acid Citric acid
Thiofentanyl/ Acetylthiofentanyl	2-Thiophene Triethylamine (TEA) 4-Piperidone monohydrate hydrochloride Diisopropylethylamine (DIPEA) Acetic anhydride	Acetic acid Mesyl chloride (MsCl) Cesium carbonate (CsCO) Sodium triacetoxyborohydride Propionyl chloride Hydrochloric acid Citric acid

Table 3.7 Cocaine

Cocaine	Precursors	Reagents
Cocaine	Cocoa leaves	Lime or cement Sodium hydroxide Sulfuric acid Hydrochloric acid Kerosene or gasoline Acetone water

Table 3.8 Gama Hydroxy Butyate (GHB)

Gama Hydroxy Butyate (GHB)	Precursors	Reagents
Gama Butyrolactone Method	γ-Butyrolactone butanediol	Sodium hydroxide, Water

Table 3.9 Heroin

Heroin	Precursors	Reagents
Heroin	Opium	Water, Calcium oxide Ammonium chloride, Acetic anhydride sodium bicarbonate Hydrochloric acid, Ammonia

Table 3.10 Phencylidine Analogs

Phencylidine analogs	Precursors	Reagents
PC1: Piperidine/ cyclohexane intermediate PC1a: Phenyl addition PC1b: Thiophene addition	Cyclohexanone Piperidine, Bromobenzene (a) Phenyl–magnesiumbromide (a) Bromothiophene (b)	Magnesium, Potassium cyanide, Sodium cyanide
PC2: Pyridine/cyclohexane intermediate PC2a: Phenyl addition PC2b: Thiophene addition	Cyclohexanone, Pyridine, Bromobenzene (a) Phenyl–magnesiumbromide (a) Bromothiophene	Magnesium, Potassium cyanide, Sodium cyanide
PC3: Morpholine/ cyclohexane intermediate PC3a: Phenyl addition PC3b: Thiophene addition	Cyclohexanone, Morpholine, Bromobenzene(a) Phenyl–magnesiumbromide (a) Bromothiophene	Magnesium, Potassium cyanide, Sodium cyanide

Table 3.11 Phenylacetone (P2P) Precursors

Phenylacetone	Precursors	Reagents
P1: P-2-P via phenylacetic acid/ acetic anhydride	Phenylacetic acid Acetic anhydride	Sodium acetate
P2: P-2-P via benzyl cyanide/ethyl acetate	Benzylcyanide	Acetic acid Phosphoric acid Sodium
	Ethyl Acetate	Sulfuric acid
P3: P-2-P via phenylacetic acid/lead acetate	Phenylacetic acid	Lead acetate
P4: P-2-P via phenylacetic acid/ acetone	Phenyl acetic acid Acetic acid	Hydrochloric acid Manganous carbonate Manganous chloride Nitric acid Pumic Sodium carbonate Thorium nitrate
P5: P-2-P via benzalbehyde/nitroethane	Benzaldehyde Nitroethane	Butylamine Ferric chloride Iron filings

Table 3.11 (Continued) Phenylacetone (P2P) Precursors

Phenylacetone	Precursors	Reagents
P6: P-2-P via phenyl-2-propanol/ dichromate	Phenyl-2-propanol	Potassium dichromate
P7: P-2-P via benzene/ chloroacetone	Benzene Chloroacetone	Aluminum chloride Sodium bisulfate

Manufacturing Method Table (Explosives)

Table 3.12 Clandestine Use Table (Explosives)

Chemical	Primary Explosives	Secondary Explosive	Black Powder	Flash Powder	Pyrotechnics
Acetic anhydride		*			
Acetone	*				
Aluminum, powder		*		*	*
Aluminum, dark pyro				*	*
Ammonia	*				
Ammonium dichromate			*		*
Ammonium nitrate	*	*	*	*	*
Ammonium perchlorate					*
Ammonium picrate			*		
Antimony, powder				*	*
Antimony trisulfide				*	*
Barium chlorate				*	*
Barium nitrate				*	*
Barium peroxide				*	*
Barium sulfate				*	*
Benzene		*		*	
Benzene hexachloride					*
Black copper oxide				*	*
Calcium hydride				*	
Calcium metal				*	
Calcium/magnesium 75/25				*	
Charcoal			*	*	*
Copper oxychloride					*
Cotton (cellulose)		*			
Dimethylaniline		*			
Glycerin		*			
Hexachlorobenzene					*
Hexachloroethane					*

(*Continued*)

Table 3.12 (Continued) Clandestine Use Table (Explosives)

Chemical	Primary Explosives	Secondary Explosive	Black Powder	Flash Powder	Pyrotechnics
Hexamethylenetetramine		*			
Hexamine		*			*
Hydrochloric acid	*				
Hydrogen peroxide	*				
Hydroxyethyl cellulose				*	
Iodine crystals	*				
Lead acetate	*				
Lead nitrate	*				
Lead peroxide					*
Lithium perchlorate				*	
Magnalium				*	*
Magnesium, powder		*		*	*
Mercury	*				
Methylaniline		*			
Nitric acid	*	*			
Petroleum jelly		*			*
Phenol		*			
Potassium chlorate		*		*	*
Potassium dichromate				*	*
Potassium iodide	*				
Potassium nitrate			*	*	*
Potassium perchlorate		*		*	
Potassium permanganate	*			*	
Potassium picrate	*		*		*
Red phosphorus	*			*	
Sodium azide	*				
Sodium chlorate					*
Sodium nitrate			*	*	*
Sodium perchlorate				*	
Starch		*	*		
Strontium nitrate				*	*
Strontium perchlorate				*	
Strontium peroxide					*
Sucrose				*	*
Sulfur			*	*	*
Sulfuric acid		*			
Titanium powder				*	*
Toluene		*			
Trichlorophenol		*		*	
Trinitroresorcinate	*				
Zinc, powder		*			*

Table 3.13 Primary Initiating Explosives

Explosive	Precursors	Reagents
Ammonium triiodide $(NH_4)I_3$	Iodine crystals Ammonia	Potassium iodide
Armstrong Mixture	Potassium chlorate red Phosphorous	
HMDT (Hexamethylene Triperoxide Diamine)	Hexamine Hydrogen peroxide	Citric acid Hydrochloric acid Sodium bicarbonate Sodium carbonate
Lead Azide $(Pb(N_3)_2)$	Lead acetate Sodium azide	
Lead Styphnate (Lead Trinitroresorcinate)	Lead nitrate Trinitroresorcinate	Magnesium oxide
Mercury Fulminate	Mercury Nitric acid	
Nitrogen Trichloride (NCl_3)	Ammonium nitrate	Hydrochloric acid Potassium permanganate
TATP (Triacetone Triperoxide)	Acetone Hydrogen peroxide	Hydrochloric Acid Sodium bicarbonate Sodium carbonate

Table 3.14 Secondary Explosives

Explosive	Precursors	Reagents
Nitrocellulose	Cotton (cellulose) Nitric acid	Sulfuric acid
Nitroglycerin	Glycerin Nitric acid	Sulfuric acid
Nitrostarch	Starch Nitric acid	Sulfuric acid
PETN (pentaerythritol tetranitrate)	Pentaerythritol Nitric acid	Sulfuric acid
Picrates	Picric acid Sodium hydroxide Potassium hydroxide Ammonia Ammonium hydroxide	
Picric Acid (2,4,6-trinitrophenol)	Phenol Nitric acid	Sulfuric acid

(Continued)

Table 3.14 (Continued) Secondary Explosives

Explosive	Precursors	Reagents
RDX (cyclonite)	Hexamine Methenamine Nitric acid Paraformaldehyde Hexamethylenetetramine	Sulfuric acid Ammonium nitrate Acetic anhydride
Tetryl (trinitro-2,4,6-phenylmethylnitramine)	Methylanine Dimethylaniline Nitric acid	Sulfuric acid
TNT (trinitro toluene)	Toluene Nitric acid	Sulfuric acid

Table 3.15 Black Powder

Black Powders	Oxidizer	Fuel
Black Powder	Potassium nitrate Sodium nitrate	Charcoal Sulfur
Black Powder Substitutes	Potassium nitrate Sodium nitrate	Charcoal Sulfur Sugar Borax Dextrin Ascorbic acid
Golden Powder® **Black Canyon®**	Potassium nitrate	Ascorbic acid
Pyrodex® and Triple Seven®	Potassium nitrate Potassium perchlorate	Sodium benzoate Dicyandiamide Charcoal Borax Dextrin Sulfur (Pyrodex) Sodium 3 nitrobenzoate (Triple Seven)

Table 3.16 Fuel Oxidizer (FOX) Mixtures

FOX Mixtures	Oxidizer	Fuel
ANAL	Ammonium nitrate	Aluminum Powder Zinc Powder
ANFO	Ammonium nitrate	Diesel Fuel Motor oil Kerosene Nitromethane

Table 3.16 (Continued) **Fuel Oxidizer (FOX) Mixtures**

FOX Mixtures	Oxidizer	Fuel
Chlorate Mixtures	Potassium chlorate Sodium chlorate	Petroleum jelly Aluminum powder Magnesium powder Sugar Zinc powder
Perchlorate Mixtures	Potassium perchlorate Sodium perchlorate	Petroleum jelly Aluminum powder Magnesium powder Sugar Zinc powder
Flash Powders	Potassium chlorate Potassium perchlorate Ammonium perchlorate Potassium nitrate Barium nitrate	Metal fuels: Al, Mg, Ti, Fe Sulfur Phosphorus Antimony sulfide Arsenic sulfide Sugar
Pyrotechnic Mixtures	Potassium chlorate Potassium perchlorate Ammonium perchlorate Potassium nitrate Barium nitrate Strontium nitrate	Sulfur Phosphorus Sawdust Wax Oil Sugar Al, Mg, Ti, Fe, Sr, Ba

Dynamite Components

Nitroglycerine
Nitrocellulose (guncotton)
Ammonium oxalate
Wood meal
Potassium nitrate
Sodium carbonate
Barium nitrate
Sodium nitrate
Starch
Potassium perchlorate
Petroleum jelly

EXPLOSIVES MANUFACTURE SCHEMES

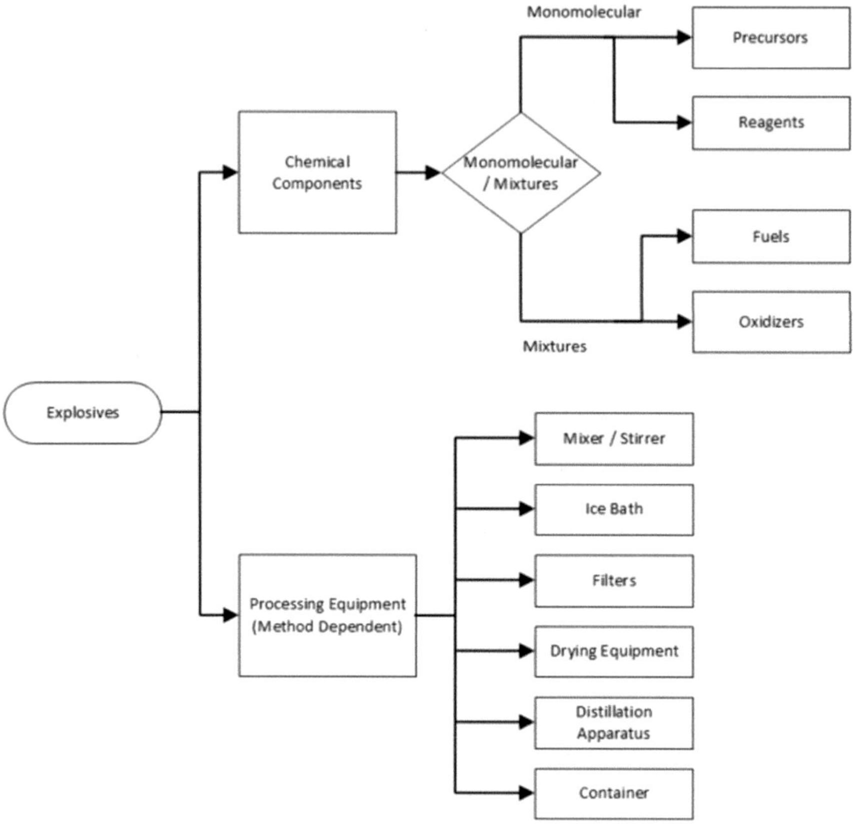

Figure 3.1 Generic Home Made Explosive (HME) Scheme.

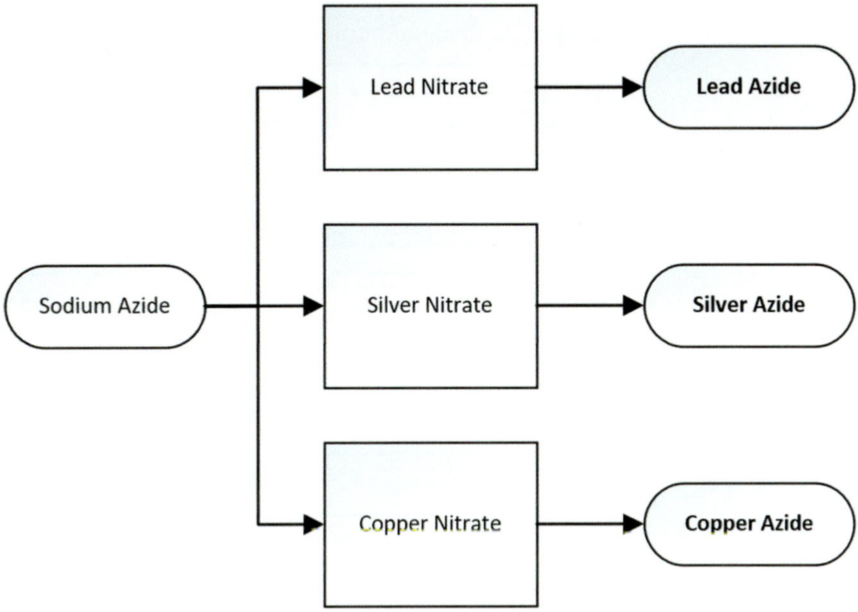

Figure 3.2 Azide (Primary) Explosives.

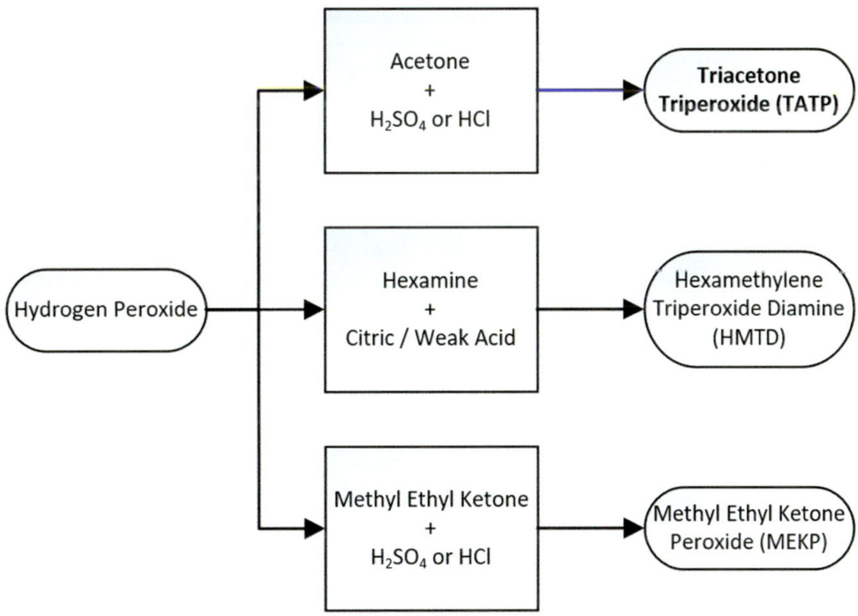

Figure 3.3 Hydrogen Peroxide Explosives.

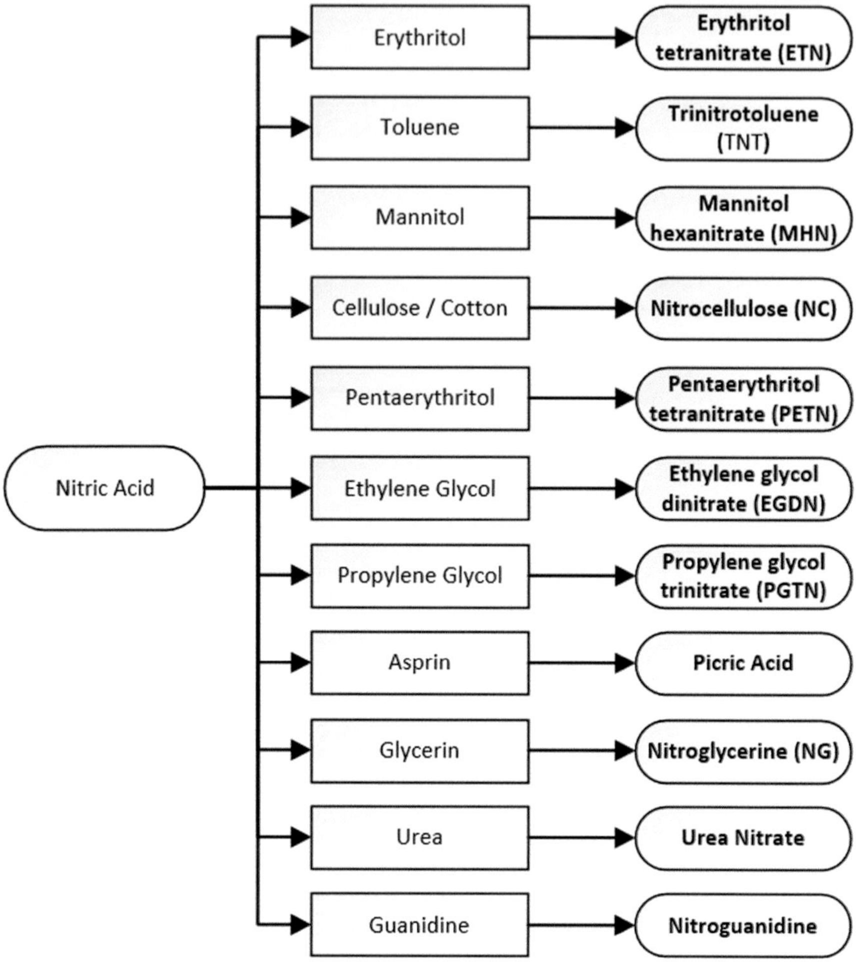

Figure 3.4 Nitrated Organic (Secondary) Explosives.

Chemical Weapons

Table 3.17 Types of Chemical Weapon

	Blood Agent	Blister Agent	Lachrymatory Agent	Irritant	Poison	Nerve Agent	Vomiting Agent	Choking Agent
Arsine	♦							
AS-20	♦							
BBC			🌢					
BC			🌢	❁				
Bromopicrin			🌢					
CA	♦		🌢		☠			
Chlorine gas					☠			
Chloropicrin					☠			
Chlorosarin						☸		
CK	♦				☠			
CN				❁				
CS				❁				
CX		♣						
DA			🌢					
DCA				❁				
DIM				❁				
DM							✱	
ED		♣						
FTH						☸		
GA						☸		
GAA						☸		
GB						☸		

(Continued)

Table 3.17 (Continued) Types of Chemical Weapon

	Blood Agent	Blister Agent	Lachrymatory Agent	Irritant	Poison	Nerve Agent	Vomiting Agent	Choking Agent
GBE						☸		
GBI						☸		
GD						☸		
GDIC						☸		
GDS						☸		
GF						☸		
GS						☸		
HC	♦				☠			
HN1		♣						
HN2		♣						
HN3		♣						
HN4		♣						
IIVX						☸		
Lewisite		♣						
MD		♣						
NPF						☸		
NPSF						☸		
PD		♣						
Phosgene								κ
Sub-VX						☸		
Sulfur Mustard		♣						
Sulfur Mustard II		♣						
VS				❁				
VX						☸		

Table 3.18 Manufacturing Method Table (Chemical Weapons)

Chemical Weapon	Ingredients
Arsine	Arsenic
	Zinc
	Hydrochloric acid
AS-20 (Phenylarsine, Diphenylarsine)	Benzene
	Arsenic trichloride
	Isopentane
	Aluminum chloride
	Sodium bicarbonate
	Sodium sulfate
BC (Cyanogen Bromide) Route 1	Sulfuric acid
	Bromine
	Sodium cyanide
BC (Cyanogen Bromide) Route 2	Sodium hydroxide
	Sodium cyanide
	Bromine
	Sulfuric acid
BC (1-Bromo-2-propanone)	Acetone
	Sulfuric acid
	Bromine
	Methylene chloride
CA (Chloroacetone) Route 1	Acetone
	Sulfuric acid
	Chlorine gas
	Methylene chloride
	Calcium chloride
CA (Chloroacetone) Route 2	Acetone
	Sulfuric acid
	Chlorine gas
	Chloroform
	Calcium chloride
CK (Cyanogen Chloride)	Sodium cyanide
	Glacial acetic acid
	Chlorine gas
	Carbon tetrachloride
DCA (1,1 Dichloroacetone)	Acetone
	Sulfuric acid
	Chlorine
	Calcium chloride
Lewisite	Acetylene
	Arsenic trichloride
	Mercuric chloride
	Hydrochloric acid

Hazard Identification

4

Figure 4.1 Physical Hazard Pictograms.

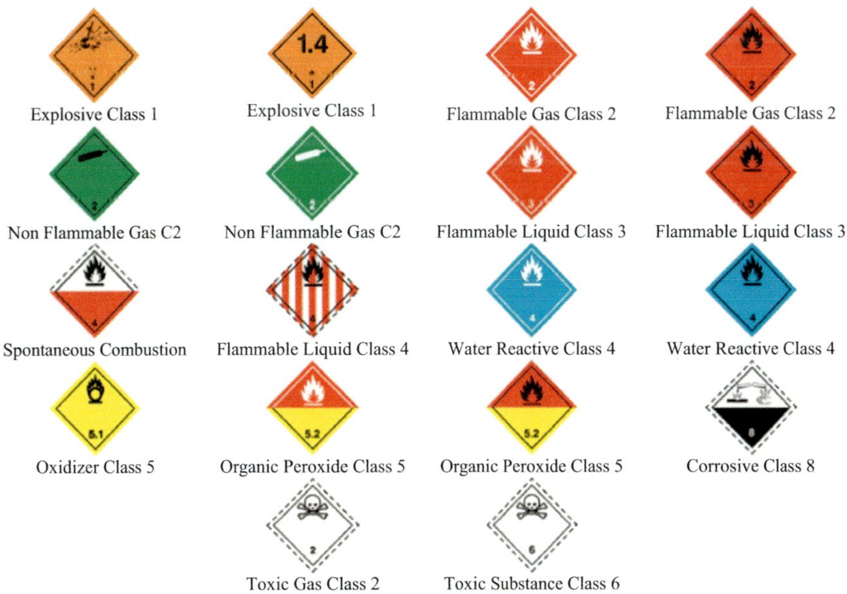

Figure 4.2 Transportation Pictograms (Placards).

DOI: 10.4324/9781003335139-4

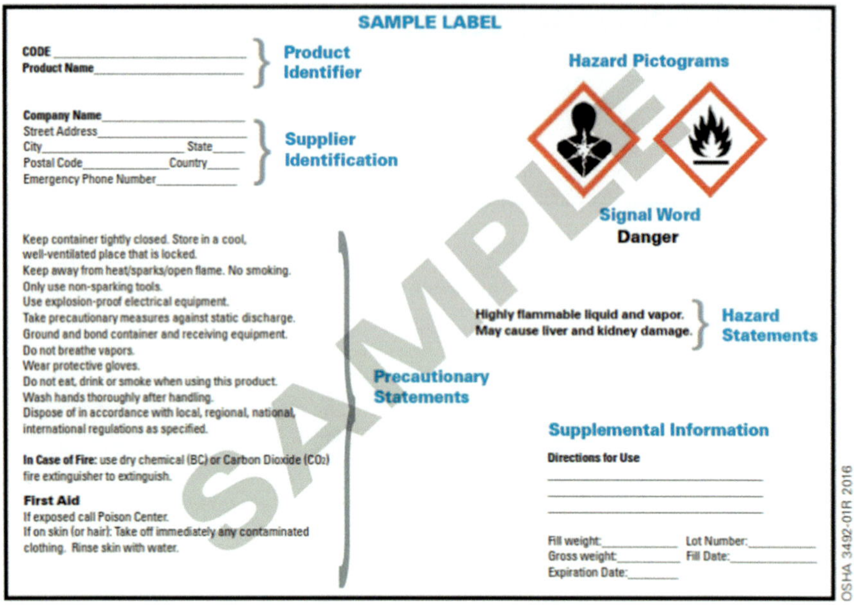

Figure 4.3 Hazard Communication Label.

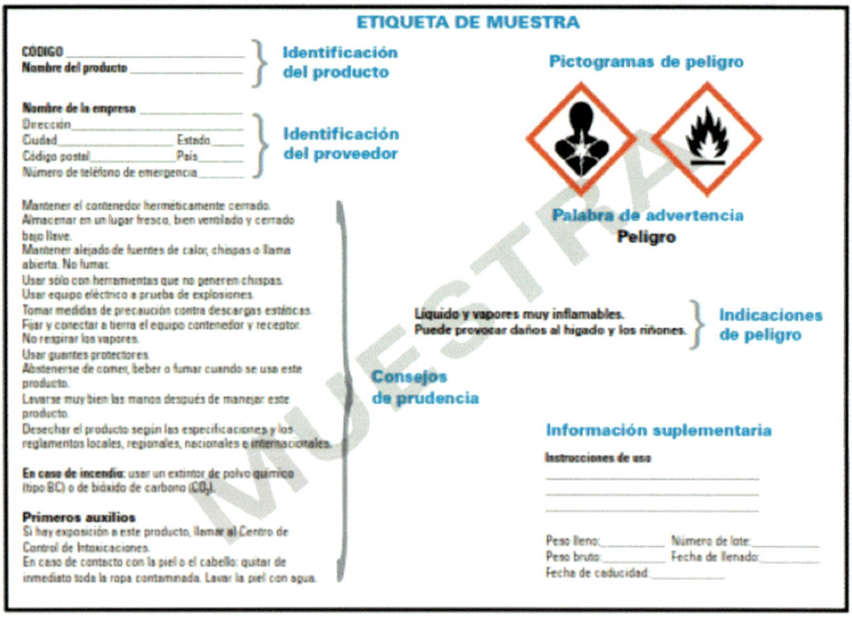

Figure 4.4 Hazard Communication Label (Spanish).

Table 4.1 Hazard Properties

Chemical	IDLH (ppm)	NIOSH REL (ppm)	OSHA PEL (ppm)	NFPA Rating	Flash Point (°F)	Explosive Limit
a,a'-Dibromo-4,4'- biacetophenone	NA	NA	NA	NA	NA	NA
Acetaldehyde	2000	NA	200	3/4/2	−6	4%/60%
Acetylene	NA	2500	NA	4/0/3	−17.8	NA
4-allyl-1,2-methylenedioxybenzene	NA	NA	NA	3/0/2	NA	NA
Acetic acid	50	10	10	3/2/0	104	4%/19.9%
Acetic anhydride	200	5	5	3/2/1	NA	2.9%/10.3%
Acetone	2500	250	1000	1/3/0	−4	2.5%/12.8%
Acetonitrile	500	20	40	2/3/0	−4	4.4%/16%
Activated charcoal	NA	NA	15 mg/m^3	2/1/1	NA	NA
Allylbenzene	NA	NA	NA	NA	177	NA
Allylchloride	250	1	1	2/3/1	30	2.9%/11.1%
Aluminum (powder)	NA	NA	15 mg/m^3	1/3/1	NA	NA
Aluminum chloride	NA	10 mg/m^3	15 mg/m^3	1/0/0	NA	15%/28%
Ammonia	300	25	50	3/1/0	NA	NA
Ammonia gas	300	25	50	NA	NA	NA
Ammonium chloride	NA	10 mg/m^3	NA	2/0/0	NA	NA
Ammonium fluoride	NA	2.5 mg/m^3	2.5 mg/m^3	3/0/1	NA	NA
Ammonium formate	NA	NA	NA	1/0/0	NA	NA
Ammonium hydroxide	NA	NA	NA	3/1/0	NA	16%/27%
Ammonium nitrate	NA	NA	NA	1/0/3 OXY	NA	NA
Ammonium oxalate	NA	NA	NA	3/0/1	NA	NA
Aniline	100	NA	5	3/2/0	158	1.3% / 11%
Antimony (powder)	NA	NA	0.5 mg/m^3	3/1/2 POI	NA	NA

(*Continued*)

Table 4.1 (Continued) Hazard Properties

Chemical	IDLH (ppm)	NIOSH REL (ppm)	OSHA PEL (ppm)	NFPA Rating	Flash Point (°F)	Explosive Limit
Antimony sulfide	NA	NA	NA	NA	NA	NA
Arsenic	5 mg As/m^3	0.002 mg As/m^3	0.010 mg As/m^3	NA	NA	NA
Arsenic trichloride	0.67	0.67	10 æg/m^3	3/0/0	NA	NA
Barium chlorate	NA	NA	NA	NA	NA	NA
Barium nitrate	NA	NA	0.5 mg/m^3	3/0/3 OXY	NA	NA
Benzaldehyde	NA	NA	NA	2/2/0	NA	1.4%/8.5%
Benzene	500	0.1	1	2/3/0	12	1.2%/7.8%
Benzyl chloride	10	1	1	3/2/1	153	1.1% / 14%
Benzyl cyanide	NA	NA	5 mg/m^3	2/1/0	223	NA
Bleach	NA	NA	0.5	2/0/1	NA	NA
Bromine	0.7	0.1	0.1	4/0/3	NA	NA
Bromobenzene	NA	NA	NA	2/2/0	NA	0.5%/2.5%
Bromoethane	NA	NA	NA	3/1/0	NA	10%/16%
Calcium chloride	NA	0.1	0.1	1/0/2	NA	NA
Carbon dioxide	40000	5000	5000	NA	NA	NA
Carbon tetrachloride	200	2	10	3/0/0	NA	NA
Charcoal	NA	NA	30.54	1/1/1	NA	0.14 g/l
Chlorine	10	0.5	1	4/0/0	NA	NA
Chlorine gas	NA	0.5	1	4/0/0	NA	NA
Chloroform	500	2	50	3/1/1/	NA	NA
Chloropicrin	0.1	0.1	0.1	4/0/3	NA	NA
2-Chloroacetyl chloride	NA	0.05	NA	3/0/2	NA	NA
Chloro-2-propanone *Chloroacetone*	NA	NA	NA	3/2/0	102	NA
Copper oxide	100 mg/m^3	1 mg/m^3	1 mg/m^3	2/1/1	NA	NA

Table 4.1 (Continued) Hazard Properties

Chemical	IDLH (ppm)	NIOSH REL (ppm)	OSHA PEL (ppm)	NFPA Rating	Flash Point (°F)	Explosive Limit
Copper sulfate	100 mg/m^3	1 mg/m^3	1 mg/m^3	2/0/0	NA	NA
Cyclohexanone	700	25	50	1/2/0	111	1.1% 9.4%
Cyclohexanol	400	50	50	2/2/1	145	NA
Dextrin	NA	NA	NA	0/2/0	NA	NA
1,10-Dibromodecane	NA	NA	NA	1/1/0	>233.6	NA
1,8-Dibromodecane	NA	NA	NA	NA	NA	NA
Dichloroethane	3000	100	100	2/3/0	>233	13%/23%
Dichloromethylphosp hine	NA	NA	NA	3/3/2	118.4	NA
Diethanolethylamine	NA	NA	NA	1/1/0	253.4	NA
Diethy ether	NA	400	400	2/4/2	−49	NA
2-Diisopropylaminoeth anol	NA	NA	NA	NA	158	NA
Dimethylamine	500	10	10	3/4/0	−58	NA
Dimethylcarbamoyl chloride	NA	NA	NA	3/2/1	155	NA
Dimethoxy ethane	NA	NA	NA	2/3/2	28	NA
Diphenylamine	NA	NA	1.44	2/1/1	302	NA
Ephedrine	NA	NA	NA	1/0/0	NA	NA
Ethyl acetate	2000	400	400	1/3/0	24	2.0%/9.0%
Ethyl alcohol	1000	1000	1000	1/3/0	61.88	NA
Ethyl chloride	3800	1000	1000	1/4/0	−58	NA
Ethylene chlorohydrin	7	5	5	4/2/0	131	NA
Ethylene dichloride	50	1	50	3/3/2	55	NA
Ethylene glycol	NA	50	50	2/2/1	232	3.2%/15.3%
2-Ethylthioethanol	NA	NA	NA	2/2/0	172.4	NA

(Continued)

Table 4.1 (Continued) Hazard Properties

Chemical	IDLH (ppm)	NIOSH REL (ppm)	OSHA PEL (ppm)	NFPA Rating	Flash Point (°F)	Explosive Limit
Formaldehyde	20	0.016	0.75	3/2/2	140	NA
Formamide	NA	10	NA	2/1/0	310	2.7%/19%
Formic acid	30	5	5	3/2/0	>233	18%/57%
Glacial acetic acid	NA	10	10	3/2/2	104	NA
Glycerin	NA	NA	3.98	1/1/0	390	NA
Glyoxal	NA	NA	NA	NA	428	NA
Hexane	5000	NA	500	1/3/0	–7	NA
Hydroiodic acid (HI)	NA	NA	NA	3/0/0	NA	NA
Hydrobromic acid (HBr)	30	3	3	3/0/0	NA	NA
Hydrochloric acid (HCl)	50	5	5	3/0/0	NA	NA
Hydrofluoric acid	NA	NA	3	4/0/2	NA	NA
Hydrogen	NA	NA	NA	0/4/0	gas	4%/75%
Hydrogen chloride	50	5	5	3/0/2	NA	NA
Hydrogen peroxide	75	1	1	3/0/1 OXY	NA	40%/100%
Hydroxylamine HCl	NA	NA	NA	3/1/1	305	NA
Iodine	NA	2	0.1	3/0/1 OXY	NA	NA
Isopentane	NA	NA	NA	2/4/0	<–60	NA
Isopropyl alcohol	2000	400	400	2/3/2	54	NA
Isopropyl ether	1400	500	500	2/3/2	–18	NA
Isopropylamine	750	NA	5	3/4/0	–34.6	NA
Isosafrole	NA	NA	NA	1/1/0	120	NA
Lead acetate	NA	0.1 mg/m^3	0.05 mg/m^3	3/0/0	NA	NA
Lithium	NA	NA	NA	1/1/2	NA	NA
Lithium aluminum hydride	NA	9.66	6.44	3/2/2 W	NA	NA

Table 4.1 (Continued) Hazard Properties

Chemical	IDLH (ppm)	NIOSH REL (ppm)	OSHA PEL (ppm)	NFPA Rating	Flash Point (°F)	Explosive Limit
Liquid bromine	NA	NA	NA	NA	NA	NA
Liquid hydrogen cyanide	NA	NA	NA	NA	−0	NA
Magnesium turnings	NA	NA	NA	0/1/2	NA	NA
Malononitril	NA	3	NA	3/1/2	233.6	NA
Manganous carbonate	NA	NA	1.06	1/0/1	NA	NA
Manganous chloride	NA	NA	NA	2/0/0	NA	NA
Mercuric chloride	0.9	0.05 mg/m^3	0.1 mg/m^3	3/0/0	NA	NA
Mercury	10 mg/m^3	0.05 mg/m^3	0.1 mg/m^3	3/0/0	NA	NA
Methanol	6000	200	200	1/3/0	54	6%/36%
Methylamine	100	10	10	3/3/0	39	4.9%/20.8%
Methyl disulfide	NA	NA	NA	3/4/0	59	NA
Methylene chloride	2,300	NA	25	3/1/2	NA	NA
Methylformamide	500	10	10	2/2/0	136	2.2%/15.2%
Methyl iodide	100	2	5	3/0/1	NA	NA
Naphthalene	500	NA	10	2/2/0	189	0.9%/5.9%
N,N-Diethylamine	30 mg/m^3	10	25	3/3/0	−18.4	NA
Neopentyl glycol	NA	NA	NA	2/1/1	224.6	NA
Nitrate trihydrate	100 mg/m^3	NA	1 mg/m^3	2/1/2	NA	NA
Nitric acid	100	2	2	4/0/3 OXY POI COR	NA	NA
Nitroethane	1000	100	100	1/3/3	82	3.4%/NA
Nitromethane	750	NA	100	2/2/4	95	NA
Norpseudoephedrine	NA	NA	NA	1/0/0	NA	NA

(Continued)

Table 4.1 (Continued) Hazard Properties

Chemical	IDLH (ppm)	NIOSH REL (ppm)	OSHA PEL (ppm)	NFPA Rating	Flash Point (°F)	Explosive Limit
O-Chlorobenzaldehyde	NA	NA	NA	NA	188.6	NA
Palladium sulfate	NA	NA	NA	NA	NA	NA
Paraffin	NA	NA	NA	1/0/0	399	NA
Pentane	NA	118.61	1000	2/4/0	−56	NA
Perchloric acid	NA	NA	NA	3/0/3 OXY	102	NA
Petroleum ether	NA	NA	300	2/4/1	0	NA
Phenol	250	5	5	3/2/1	175	1.8%/8.6%
Phenylacetic acid	NA	NA	NA	2/0/0	168	NA
Phosphorus	5 mg/m^3	0.1 mg/m^3	0.1 mg/m^3	1/1/1	NA	NA
Phosphorus pentachloride	8.22	0.12	0.12	3/0/2 W	NA	NA
Phosphorous trichloride	25	0.2	0.5	4/0/2	NA	NA
Phosphorus oxytrichloride	NA	NA	NA	4/0/3	NA	NA
Pinacolyl alcohol	NA	NA	NA	1/3/0	78.8	NA
Piperidine	NA	NA	NA	2/3/3	60.8	NA
Piperonal	NA	NA	NA	1/0/0	NA	NA
Platinum catalyst	NA	1 mg/m^3	NA	2/2/1	NA	NA
Platinum chloride	NA	NA	NA	2/0/0	NA	NA
Platinum oxide	NA	NA	NA	2/0/0	NA	NA
Potassium carbonate	NA	NA	NA	2/0/0	NA	NA
Potassium chlorate	NA	NA	NA	1/0/3 OXY	NA	NA
Potassium cyanide	9.39	1.88	1.88	3/0/0	NA	NA
Potassium dichromate	NA	NA	NA	3/1/1 OXY	NA	NA
Potassium ferro cyanide	NA	NA	NA	1/0/2	NA	NA
Potassium hydroxide	ND	0.87	ND	3/0/1	NA	NA

Table 4.1 (Continued) Hazard Properties

Chemical	IDLH (ppm)	NIOSH REL (ppm)	OSHA PEL (ppm)	NFPA Rating	Flash Point (°F)	Explosive Limit
Potassium nitrate	NA	NA	NA	1/0/0 OXY	NA	NA
Potassium perchlorate	NA	NA	NA	2/0/0 OXY	NA	NA
Potassium permanganate	NA	NA	0.77	1/0/0 OXY	NA	NA
Powdered tin	NA	2 mg/m^3	NA	NA	NA	NA
Propylene chlorohydrin	NA	NA	NA	NA	NA	NA
Pyridine	1000	5	5	2/3/0	68	1.8%/12.4%
3-Pyridol	NA	NA	NA	NA	343	NA
Pyrolidine	NA	NA	NA	NA	NA	NA
Rhombic sulfur	NA	NA	NA	NA	NA	NA
Silica Gel	NA	6 mg/m^3	15 mg/m^3	2/1/1	NA	NA
Silver nitrate	NA	NA	NA	1/0/0 OXY	NA	NA
Sodium	NA	NA	NA	3/3/2 W	NA	NA
Sodium acetate	NA	NA	NA	3/0/1	NA	NA
Sodium azide	NA	0.1	NA	3/1/3 POI EXPL	NA	NA
Sodium bicarbonate	NA	NA	NA	1/1/1	NA	NA
Sodium bisulfate	NA	NA	NA	2/0/1	NA	NA
Sodium carbonate	NA	NA	NA	1/0/1	NA	NA
Sodium chlorate	NA	NA	NA	1/0/1 OXY	NA	NA
Sodium chloride	NA	NA	NA	1/0/0	NA	NA
Sodium cyanide	NA	4.7	2.49 skin	3/0/2	NA	NA
Sodium ferro cyanide	NA	NA	NA	NA	NA	NA
Sodium fluoride	NA	NA	2.5 $mg(F)/m^3$	3/0/1	NA	NA
Sodium hydroxide	6.11	1.22	1.22	3/0/2	NA	NA

(Continued)

Table 4.1 (Continued) Hazard Properties

Chemical	IDLH (ppm)	NIOSH REL (ppm)	OSHA PEL (ppm)	NFPA Rating	Flash Point (°F)	Explosive Limit
Sodium sulfide monohydride	NA	NA	NA	NA	NA	NA
Sodium peroxide	NA	NA	NA	3/0/1 OXY	NA	NA
Sulfur trioxide	NA	NA	NA	3/0/2	NA	NA
Sodium sulfate	NA	NA	NA	1/0/0	NA	NA
Starch	NA	10 mg/m^3	15 mg/m^3	0/1/0	NA	NA
Strontium nitrate	NA	NA	NA	1/0/3 OXY	NA	NA
Sulfur	NA	NA	NA	2/1/0	NA	NA
Sulfuric acid	15	1	1	3/0/3	NA	NA
Tetraethyl lead	40 mg Pb/m^3 [Unch]	0.075 mg/m^3	0.075 mg/m^3	NA	NA	NA
Tetrahydrofuran	2000	200	200	2/3/2	7	NA
Thionyl chloride	NA	1	NA	4/0/2	NA	NA
Thiophosphorus trichloride	NA	NA	NA	NA	NA	NA
Thorium nitrate	NA	NA	NA	NA	NA	NA
Toluene	500	100	200	2/3/0	43	3.3%/19%
Tributanolamine	NA	NA	NA	NA	NA	NA
Triethanolamine	NA	NA	25	2/1/1	354	NA
Triylmethylamine	NA	10	NA	NA	21.2	NA
Xylene	900	100	100	2/3/0	90	1.0%/7.0%
Zinc (powder)	NA	NA	NA	0/1/1	NA	NA

Table 4.2 Chemical Incompatibilities

Chemical	Incompatibilities
a,a'-Dibromo-4,4'-biacetophenone	N/A
Acetaldehyde	Strong oxidizers, acids, bases, alcohols, ammonia and amines, phenols, ketones, HCN, H2S (Note: Prolonged contact with air may cause formation of peroxides that may explode and burst containers; easily undergoes polymerization.)
Acetylene	Copper, silver, and mercury **Conditions to avoid:** Mechanical shock and high temperatures
4-allyl-1,2-methylenedioxybenzene	Water, organic materials, aluminum chloride reacts violently with water producing hydrochloric acid and heat.
Acetic acid	Chromic acid, nitric acid, ethylene glycol, perchloric acid, phosphorous trichloride, oxidizers, sodium peroxide, strong caustics, most metals (except aluminum), carbonates, hydroxides, oxides, and phosphates **Conditions to avoid:** Heat, flame, ignition sources, freezing
Acetic anhydride	Water, steam, mineral acids, oxidizing materials, alcohols, or amines may cause violent reaction. Contact with strong caustics will cause violent reaction and spattering. Corrosive to copper, brass, bronze, and iron. **Conditions to avoid:** Heat, flames, ignition sources, water
Acetone	Concentrated nitric and sulfuric acid mixtures, oxidizing materials, chloroform, alkalis, chlorine compounds, acids, potassium t-butoxide **Conditions to avoid:** Heat, flames, ignition sources
Acetonitrile	Oxidizing materials, sulfuric acid, oleum, chlorosulfonic acid, n-fluoro compounds, nitrating agents, and perchlorates **Conditions to avoid:** Heat, flames, ignition sources
Activated charcoal	Strong oxidizers such as ozone, liquid oxygen, chlorine, permanganate, etc. may result in rapid combustion **Conditions to avoid:** Moisture and strong acids
Allylbenzene	NA
Allylchloride	Explosion hazard when exposed to acids or oxidizing agents, Explosive reaction with alkyl aluminum chlorides + aromatic hydrocarbons (e.g., benzene or toluene). Violently exothermic polymerization reaction with Lewis acids (e.g., aluminum chloride, boron trifluoride, and sulfuric acid).

(Continued)

Table 4.2 (Continued) Chemical Incompatibilities

Chemical	Incompatibilities
	Incompatible with ethylene imine, ethylenediamine, chlorosulfonic acid, oleum, sodium hydroxide, and nitric acid.
Aluminum (powder)	Mercury, halocarbons, halogens, water (with bulk aluminum powder) strong oxidizing agents, some acids, and bases **Conditions to avoid:** Moisture, heat, flames, ignition sources
Aluminum chloride	Water, moist air **Conditions to avoid:** Moisture
Ammonia	Mercury, chlorine, calcium hypochlorite, hydrofluoric acid (anhydrous), bromine pentaflouride, chlorine trifluoride, chloroformates, strong acids, strong oxidizing agents, brass, zinc, aluminum, copper, bronze, most common metals, and dimethyl sulfate. Corrosive to copper, zinc, and many metal surfaces. Reacts with hypochlorite or other halogen sources to form explosive compounds that are sensitive to pressure or increases in temperature. Reaction with sulfuric acid or other strong mineral acids is exothermic; mixture becomes boiling hot. **Conditions to avoid:** Heat, direct sunlight
Ammonia gas	Strong acids and bases
Ammonium chloride	Concentrated acids, strong bases, silver salts, potassium chlorate, ammonium nitrate, bromine trifluoride, and iodine heptafluoride. Ammonium chloride reacts explosively with potassium chlorate or bromine trifluoride, and violently with bromide pentafluoride, ammonium compounds, nitrates, and iodine heptafluoride. Explosive nitrogen trichloride may result from reaction of ammonium chloride and hydrogen cyanide. **Conditions to avoid:** Heat, moisture
Ammonium fluoride	Strong oxidizing agents, strong acids, strong bases, metals **Conditions to avoid:** Dust generation, excess heat, exposure to moist air or water
Ammonium formate	**Conditions to avoid:** Heat and moisture
Ammonium hydroxide	Acids, acrolein, dimethyl sulfate, halogens, silver nitrate, propylene oxide, nitromethane, silver oxide, silver permanganate, oleum, beta-propiolactone **Conditions to avoid:** Heat, sunlight, sources of ignition

Table 4.2 (Continued) Chemical Incompatibilities

Chemical	Incompatibilities
Ammonium nitrate	Aluminum, antimony, chromium, copper, iron, lead, magnesium, manganese, nickel, zinc, brass, oil, charcoal, organic material, acetic acid, ammonium chloride, bismuth, cadmium, chlorides, cobalt, phosphorus, potassium and ammonium sulfate, sodium, sodium hypochlorite, sodium perchlorate, sodium-potassium alloy, and sulfur **Conditions to avoid:** Heat, flame, ignition sources, dusting. Moisture and combustible materials. Shock sensitive.
Ammonium oxalate	Sodium hypochlorite plus ammonium acetate, strong acids **Conditions to avoid:** Heat
Aniline	Strong acids and strong oxidizers, albumin, solutions of iron, zinc, aluminum, toluene diisocyanate, and alkalis. Ignites spontaneously in the presence of red fuming nitric acid, and with sodium. **Conditions to avoid:** Heat, flames, ignition sources
Antimony (powder)	Strong oxidizing agents, strong acids, halogen acids, chlorine, fluorine **Conditions to avoid:** Heat, Light
Antimony sulfide	Strong oxidizing agents. Avoid contact with acid.
Arsenic	Reactive with oxidizing agents, acids, moisture
Arsenic trichloride	Potassium, sodium, and aluminum
Barium chlorate	Heat, strong acids, reducing agents, finely powdered metals, aluminum
Barium nitrate	Magnesium plus barium oxide plus zinc, aluminum and magnesium alloys, combustibles (paper, oil, wood), acids, and oxidizers. Mixtures with finely divided aluminum-magnesium alloys are easily ignitable and extremely sensitive to friction or impact. **Conditions to avoid:** Heat, dusting, contact with combustibles
Benzaldehyde	Performic acid and other oxidizing materials **Conditions to avoid:** Heat, flames, ignition sources
Benzene	Strong oxidizers, many fluorides and perchlorates, nitric acid
Benzyl chloride	Water, dimethyl sulfoxide, oxidizing material, steam **Conditions to avoid:** Heat, flames, ignition sources

(*Continued*)

Table 4.2 (Continued) Chemical Incompatibilities

Chemical	Incompatibilities
Benzyl cyanide	Strong acids, strong bases, strong oxidizing agents, strong reducing agents, sodium hypochlorite
Bleach	Ammonia (chloramine gas may evolve), amines, ammonium salts, aziridine, methanol, phenyl acetonitrile, cellulose, ethyleneimine, oxidizable metals, acids, soaps, and bisulfates
Bromine	Reducing agents, alkalies, chemically active metals, combustible materials
	Conditions to avoid:
	Moisture, heat, flames, ignition sources, and avoid direct sunlight.
Bromobenzene	Strong oxidizers
	Conditions to avoid:
	Heat, flames, ignition sources
Bromoethane	Risk of fire and explosion on contact with aluminum, zinc, or magnesium
Calcium chloride	Bromine trifluoride, furan-2-peroxycarboxylic acid
Carbon dioxide	Dusts of various metals, such as magnesium, zirconium, titanium, aluminum, chromium, and manganese, are ignitable and explosive when suspended in carbon dioxide; forms carbonic acid in water.
Carbon tetrachloride	Aluminum, bromine trifluoride, calcium hypochlorite, dimethyl formamide, ethylene oxide, fluorine, lithium, magnesium, potassium, potassium-tert- butoxide, silver perchlorate, sodium, uranium, chlorine trifluoride, dinitrogen tetraoxide, methanol
Charcoal	Strong oxidizers such as ozone, liquid oxygen, chlorine, permanganate, etc. may result in rapid combustion
	Conditions to avoid:
	Moisture, strong acids
2-Chloroacetyl chloride	Alcohols, strong bases
Chlorine	Hydrocarbons, ammonia, ether, hydrogen, acetylene, turpentine, powdered metals, and other reducing agents
Chlorine gas	Combustible materials, bases, metals, halogens, metal salts, reducing agents, amines, metal carbide, metal oxides. Oxidizing material, halo carbons, acids
	Condition to Avoid:
	Intense local heat
Chloroform	Strong oxidizing agents, aluminum, fluorine, magnesium, sodium potassium, lithium, caustics (e.g., ammonia, ammonium hydroxide, calcium hydroxide, potassium hydroxide, sodium hydroxide), dinitrogen tetraoxide, sodium + methanol, potassium-tert-butoxide, chemically active metals, Attacks some forms of plastics, rubbers, and

Table 4.2 (Continued) Chemical Incompatibilities

Chemical	Incompatibilities
	coatings., nitrogen tetraoxide, acetone + alkali, disilane, perchloric acid + phosphorus pentoxide, sodium methylate, triisopropylphosphine, sodium methoxide + methanol **Conditions to avoid:** Light, heat, air
Chloropicrin	Strong bases, aluminum, amines, magnesium, sodium methoxide, aniline, aluminum alloys, magnesium alloys, 3-bromopropyne, alcoholic sodium hydroxide, propargyl bromide **Conditions to avoid:** Excess heat
Chloro-2-propanone (chloroacetone)	Strong acids, strong bases, strong oxidizing agents, strong reducing agents
Copper oxide	Aluminum, boron, cesium acetylene carbide, dirubidium acetylide, hydrazine, hydrogen, hydrogen sulfide, lead oxide, magnesium, metals, phospham, potassium, phthalic anhydride, rubidium acetylene carbide, sodium, titanium, and zirconium; forms acetylides with acetylene, sodium hypobromite, and nitromethane.
Copper sulfate	Substance will ignite hydroxylamine. Solutions are acidic and can react with magnesium to evolve flammable hydrogen gas. May react with acetylene to form dangerous acetylides.
Cyclohexanol	Oxidizing agents **Conditions to avoid:** Heat, flame, ignition sources, temperatures below 77°F
Cyclohexanone	Strong oxidizing agents. May cause spontaneous ignition and violent reaction. May attack plastics, resins, and rubber. **Conditions to avoid:** Heat, flames, ignition sources
Dextrin	Strong oxidizers **Conditions to avoid:** Heat, flames, ignition sources
1,10-Dibromodecane	Strong bases
1,8-Dibromodecane	N/A
Dichloroethane	Aluminum or magnesium powder, oxidizing agents, reducing agents, organic peroxides, alkali and alkali earth metals, nitric acid, caustics, nitrogen tetraoxide, ammonia, and dimethylaminopropylamine **Conditions to avoid:** Heat, flame, sources of ignition, light

(Continued)

Table 4.2 (Continued) Chemical Incompatibilities

Chemical	Incompatibilities
Dichloromethylphosphine	Water, strong oxidizing agents, strong bases, air **Conditions to avoid:** Ignition sources, exposure to air, excess heat, strong oxidants, exposure to moist air or water
2-Diisopropylaminoethanol	N/A
Diethanolethylamine	Oxidizing agents
Diethy ether	Acetyl peroxide, liquid oxygen, bromoazide, chlorine, and strong oxidizers such as nitrates. Avoid heat, flame, other sources of ignition, and exposure to light, air **Conditions to avoid:** Heat, flame, ignition sources, light, and air
2-Dimethylaminomethanol	N/A
Dimethylamine	Mercury, silver, copper and its alloys, tin commercial nickel, zinc and its alloys, perchlorates, nitrates, permanganates, nitric acid, chlormates, halogens and peroxides
Dimethylcarbamoyl chloride	Oxidizing agents, alcohols strong bases, and amines
Dimethoxy ethane	Strong oxidizers
Diphenylamine	Hexachloromelamine, trichloromelamine, and oxidizing agents **Conditions to avoid:** Light and heat
Ephedrine	Oxidizing agents, direct light
Ethyl acetate	Avoid heat, flame, and other sources of ignition. Contact with nitrates, strong oxidizers, strong alkalis, or strong acids may cause fire and explosions. Will attack some forms of plastic, rubber, and coatings.
Ethyl alcohol	Strong oxidizing agents, acids, alkali metals, ammonia, hydrazine, peroxides, sodium, acid anhydrides, calcium hypochlorite, chromyl chloride, nitrosyl perchlorate, bromine pentafluoride, perchloric acid, silver nitrate, mercuric nitrate, potassium-tert-butoxide, magnesium perchlorate, acid chlorides, platinum, uranium hexafluoride, silver oxide, iodine heptafluoride, acetyl bromide, disulfuryl difluoride, tetrachlorosilane + water, acetyl chloride, permanganic acid, ruthenium (VIII) oxide, uranyl perchlorate, potassium dioxide. **Conditions to avoid:** Ignition sources, excess heat, oxidizers
Ethyl chloride	N/A
Ethylene chlorohydrin	Strong oxidizing agents, strong acids, strong bases

Table 4.2 (Continued) Chemical Incompatibilities

Chemical	Incompatibilities
Ethylene dichloride	Aluminum or magnesium powder, oxidizing agents, reducing agents, organic peroxides, alkali and alkali earth metals, nitric acid, caustics, nitrogen tetraoxide, ammonia, and dimethylaminopropylamine **Conditions to avoid:** Heat, flame, sources of ignition, light
Ethylene glycol	Strong oxidizing agents. Reacts violently with chlorosulfonic acid, oleum, sulfuric acid, perchloric acid. Causes ignition at room temperature with chromium trioxide, potassium permanganate, and sodium peroxide; causes ignition at 212°F(100°C) with ammonium dichromate, silver chlorate, sodium chloride, and uranyl nitrate. **Conditions to avoid:** Heat, flames, ignition sources, water (absorbs readily)
2-Ethylthioethanol	N/A
Formaldehyde	Oxidizing agents and alkalis. Reacts explosively with nitrogen dioxide at ca. 180°C (356°F). Reacts violently with perchloric acid, perchloric acid-aniline acid may form bis-chloromethyl ether, mixtures, and nitromethane. Reaction with hydrochloric an OSHA regulated carcinogen. **Conditions to avoid:** Heat, flames, ignition sources
Formamide	Acids, alkalines, iodine, pyridine, and sulfur trioxide. Copper, brass, lead, and rubber are attacked by formamide. **Conditions to avoid:** Heat, flames, ignition sources
Formic acid	Sulfuric acid, strong caustics, furfuryl alcohol, hydrogen peroxide, strong oxidizers, and bases. Reacts explosively with oxidizing agents. **Conditions to avoid:** Heat, flame, other sources of ignition
Glacial acetic acid	Acetic acid is incompatible with chromic acid, nitric acid, ethylene glycol, perchloric acid, phosphorous trichloride, oxidizers, sodium peroxide, strong caustics, most metals (except aluminum), carbonates, hydroxides, oxides, and phosphates. **Conditions to avoid:** Heat, flame, ignition sources, freezing
Glycerin	Strong oxidizers. Can react violently with acetic anhydride, calcium oxychloride, chromium oxides and alkali metal hydrides. **Conditions to avoid:** Heat, flames, ignition sources
Glyoxal	N/A

(Continued)

Table 4.2 (Continued) Chemical Incompatibilities

Chemical	Incompatibilities
Hexane	Oxygen and other oxidizers **Conditions to avoid:** Heat, flames, ignition sources
Hydrofluoric acid	Arsenic trioxide, phosphorus pentoxide, ammonia, calcium oxide, sodium hydroxide, sulfuric acid, vinyl acetate, ethylenediamine, acetic anhydride, alkalis, organic materials, most common metals, rubber, leather, water, strong bases, carbonates, sulfides, cyanides, oxides of silicon, especially glass, concrete, silica **Conditions to avoid:** Moisture
Hydroiodic acid (HI)	Strong oxidizers, alkalis, fluorine, potassium, nitric acid, some metals, water, and steam. Attacks natural rubber. **Conditions to avoid:** Light, heat
Hydrobromic acid (HBr)	Reacts violently with fluorine gas, ammonia, ozone, ferric oxide, alkalis, metals and strong oxidizing agents. **Conditions to avoid:** Light, heat, air
Hydrochloric acid (HCl)	Highly reactive with strong bases, metals, metal oxides, hydroxides, amines, carbonates and other alkaline materials. Incompatible with materials such as cyanides, sulfides, sulfites, and formaldehyde. **Conditions to avoid:** Heat, direct sunlight
Hydrogen	Oxidizing agents, some metals, alkaline material, halogens
Hydrogen chloride	Highly reactive with strong bases, metals, metal oxides, hydroxides, amines, carbonates and other alkaline materials. Incompatible with materials such as cyanides, sulfides, sulfites, and formaldehyde. **Conditions to avoid:** Heat, direct sunlight
Hydrogen peroxide	Heat, reducing agents, organic materials, dirt, alkalis, rust, and many metals. Spontaneous combustion may occur on standing in contact with readily flammable materials. **Conditions to avoid:** Light. Avoid excess heat and contact with combustible or organic materials.
Hydroxylamine HCl	Strong oxidizing agents, heat plus sodium acetate or ether, carbonyl compounds, copper sulfate, zinc and phosphorus chlorides. **Conditions to avoid:** Heat, flame, moisture, dusting, sources of ignition and shock

Table 4.2 (Continued) Chemical Incompatibilities

Chemical	Incompatibilities
Iodine	Ammonia, powdered metals, alkali metals, or strong reducing agents. Reaction can be violent or explosive with acetaldehyde and acetylene. Reacts with ammonium hydroxide to form shock-sensitive iodides on drying. **Conditions to avoid:** Heat, sunlight, and poor ventilation
Isopentane	Oxidizing materials **Conditions to avoid:** Heat, flame, and other sources of ignitions
Isopropyl alcohol	Heat, flame, strong oxidizers, acetaldehyde, acids, chlorine, ethylene oxide, hydrogen-palladium combination, hydrogen peroxide-sulfuric acid combination, potassium tert-butoxide, hypochlorous acid, isocyanates, nitroform, phosgene, aluminum, oleum and perchloric acid. **Conditions to avoid:** Heat, flames, ignition sources
Isopropylamine	Strong oxidizing agents, strong acids **Conditions to avoid:** High temperatures, ignition sources, confined spaces
Isopropyl ether	Air, oxygen, chlorosulfonic acid, nitric acid. Contact with oxidizers may cause explosions or fire. **Conditions to avoid:** Heat, flames, ignition sources
Isosafrole	Oxidizing agents
Lead acetate	Bromates, phenol, chloral hydrate, sulfides, hydrogen peroxide, resorcinol, salicylic acid, sulfites, vegetable infusions, alkalis, tannin, phosphates, citrates, chlorides, carbonates, tartrates, and acids **Conditions to avoid:** Heat, flames, ignition sources
Lithium	Moisture, acids, oxidizers, oxygen, nitrogen, carbon dioxide
Lithium aluminum hydride	Heat, water, alcohols, acids, transition metal salts, oxidizing agents, and a wide variety of other substances. Violent reacts occur on contact with powerful oxidizers. Exothermic reactions involving hydrogen occur when heated or in contact with moisture or acids. **Conditions to avoid:** Moisture, heat, flames, ignition sources
Liquid bromine	Reactive with reducing agents, combustible materials, and organic materials.
Liquid hydrogen cyanide	N/A

(Continued)

Table 4.2 (Continued) Chemical Incompatibilities

Chemical	Incompatibilities
Magnesium turnings	Oxidizers, carbonates, cyanides, chlorinated hydrocarbons, sulfates, acids, and other metals. Reacts with acids to form hydrogen gas. **Conditions to avoid:** Moisture, heat, flames, ignition sources
Malononitril	Strong oxidizing agents, strong reducing agents, strong acids, strong bases. **Conditions to avoid:** Dust generation, excess heat, temperatures above 130°C.
Manganous carbonate	Contact with acids may generate carbon dioxide gas. Oxidizes toxic sulfur dioxide to the more toxic sulfur trioxide and causes violent decomposition of hydrogen peroxide. **Conditions to avoid:** Excessive dust generation
Manganous chloride	Strong reducing agents, hydrogen peroxide, potassium, sodium, and zinc
Mercuric chloride	Bromides, iodides, ammonia, alkalis, cyanides, chlorides, copper and lead salts, silver salts, carbonates, sulfides, soap, lime water, iodoform, and hydrogen peroxide **Conditions to avoid:** Light
Mercury	Acetylenes, ammonia, ethylene oxide, chlorine dioxide, azides, metal oxides, methyl silane, lithium, rubidium, oxygen, strong oxidants, and metal carbonyls **Conditions to avoid:** Heat, flames, ignition sources, metal surfaces
Methanol	Strong oxidizing agents such as nitrates, perchlorates, or sulfuric acid. Will attack some forms of plastics, rubber, and coatings. May react with metallic aluminum and generate hydrogen gas. **Conditions to avoid:** Heat, flames, ignition sources
Methylamine	Nitromethane, acids, oxidizing agents, chlorine, hypochlorite, halogenated agents, mercury, copper, copper alloys, zinc, zinc alloys, aluminum, perchlorates
Methyl disulfide	Oxidizing agents may react with copper, rubber, and plastic **Conditions to avoid:** Ignition sources, excess heat, strong oxidants
Methylene chloride	Strong oxidizers, strong caustics, plastics, rubber, nitric acid, water + heat, and chemically active metals, such as aluminum and magnesium powder, sodium, potassium,

Table 4.2 (Continued) Chemical Incompatibilities

Chemical	Incompatibilities
	and lithium. Avoid contact with open flames and electrical arcs. Liquid methylene chloride will attack some forms of plastics, rubber, and coatings. **Conditions to avoid:** Moisture, heat, flames, ignition sources
Methylformamide	Bromine, carbon tetrachloride, chromic anhydride, 2,5-dimethylpyrrole, phosphorus oxychloride, hexachlorobenzene, magnesium nitrate, methylene diisocyanate, phosphorus trioxide, triethyl aluminum, organic nitrates, acidic and alkaline materials, and other halogenated compounds. Contact with iron or strong oxidizers may cause fires and explosions; may react violently with alkyl aluminums. Methylene diisocyanate can polymerize violently on contact with DMF. **Conditions to avoid:** Heat, flames, ignition sources
Methyl iodide	Strong oxidizers, powdered metals, reducing agents
N,N-Diethylamine	Strong oxidizing agents, acids, epichlorohydrin, cellulose nitrate, some metals.
Naphthalene	Strong oxidizers, strong alkalis and strong mineral acids, mixtures of aluminum trichloride and benzoyl chloride. Reacts violently with chromic anhydride. Melted naphthalene will attack some forms of plastics, rubber, and coatings. **Conditions to avoid:** Avoid heat, sparks, flames and other ignition sources
Neopentyl glycol	Acid chlorides, strong oxidizing agents, acid anhydrides
Nitrate trihydrate	Strong oxidizing agents, ammonia, anhydrides, amides, cyanides (e.g., potassium cyanide, sodium cyanide) **Conditions to avoid:** Combustible material, reducing agents, strong oxidants, and organic matter
Nitromethane	Amines, acids, bases, oxidizing materials, metal oxides, aluminum chloride plus organic matter, hexamethylbenzene, hydrocarbons, calcium hypochlorite, potassium hydroxide, sodium hydroxide, calcium hydroxide. Slowly corrodes steel and copper when wet. Nitromethane in the presence of water can react with organic bases to form salts which are explosive when dry. **Conditions to avoid:** Heat, flames, ignition sources; shock sensitive
Nitric acid	Especially strong bases, metallic powders, carbides, hydrogen sulfide, turpentine, and combustible organics

(Continued)

Table 4.2 (Continued) Chemical Incompatibilities

Chemical	Incompatibilities
	Conditions to avoid:
	Heat, light, moisture
Nitroethane	Amines; strong acids, alkalis and oxidizers; hydrocarbons; combustibles; metal oxides
Norpseudoephedrine	Oxidizing agents, direct light
o-Chlorobenzaldehyde	Oxidizing agents, reducing agents, bases
Palladium sulfate	Strong oxidizing agents
	Conditions to avoid:
	Freezing
Paraffin	Strong oxidizing agents
	Conditions to avoid:
	Heat, flame, other sources of ignition
Pentane	Strong oxidizers
	Conditions to avoid:
	Heat, flames, ignition sources
Perchloric acid	Combustible materials, organic chemicals, strong dehydrating agents, reducing and oxidizing agents. Reacts violently with benzene, calcium hydride, wood, acetic acid, charcoal, olefins, ethanol, sulfur, and sulfuric acid.
	Conditions to avoid:
	Heat
Petroleum ether	Strong oxidizers. Will attack some forms of plastics, rubber, and coatings.
	Conditions to avoid:
	Heat, flame, ignition sources, sunlight
Phenol	Oxidizers, aluminum chloride and nitrobenzene, calcium hypochlorite, butadiene, halogens, formaldehyde, mineral oxidizing acids, isocyanates, sodium nitrite and many other materials. Hot liquid phenol will attack aluminum, magnesium, lead, and zinc metals
	Conditions to avoid:
	Heat, flames, ignition sources
Phenylacetic acid	NA
Phosphorus	Halogens, halides, sulfur, oxidizing materials, and alkalis (forms phosphine)
	Conditions to avoid:
	Heat, flame, ignition sources, shock, friction
Phosphorus pentachloride	Reacts violently with water. Alcohols, amines, aluminum, sodium, potassium acids.
Phosphorous trichloride	Water and water vapor
Phosphorus oxytrichloride	Carbon disulfide, DMF, water, combustible materials, most common metals (except nickel and lead), alcohols, amines, and dimethyl sulfoxide

Table 4.2 (Continued) Chemical Incompatibilities

Chemical	Incompatibilities
	Conditions to avoid:
	Moisture
Pinacolyl alcohol	Oxidizing agents
Piperidine	Acids; acid chlorides; acid anhydrides; carbon dioxide; strong oxidizing agents; dicyanofurazan; N-nitrosoacetanilide; 1-perchlorylpiperdine
Piperonal	Strong oxidizing agents
Platinum catalyst	Aluminum, acetone, arsenic, ethane, hydrazine, hydrogen peroxide, lithium, phosphorus, selenium, tellurium, various fluorides
Platinum chloride	Bromine trifluoride, carbonates, sulfides and cyanides
	Conditions to avoid:
	Moisture, light, heat
Platinum oxide	Oxidizing agents
	Conditions to avoid:
	Moisture, light, heat
Potassium carbonate	Acids, chlorine trifluoride, magnesium. An explosion occurred after mixing sodium hydrosulfite, aluminum powder, potassium carbonate, and benzaldehyde
	Conditions to avoid:
	Moisture, heat, dusting
Potassium chlorate	Iodides, tartaric acid, aluminum, sulfuric acid, hypophosphite, powdered metals, organic matter, and many other oxidizable substances
	Conditions to avoid:
	Heat, flame, ignition sources, shock, friction
Potassium cyanide	Strong acids and strong oxidizers. Reacts with acids to liberate toxic and flammable hydrogen cyanide gas. Water or weak alkaline solutions can produce dangerous amounts of hydrogen cyanide in confined areas. Can react with carbon dioxide in ordinary air to form hydrogen cyanide gas.
	Conditions to avoid:
	Heat, moisture
Potassium dichromate	Reducing agents, acetone plus sulfuric acid, boron plus silicon, ethylene glycol, iron, hydrazine, and hydroxylamine. Any combustible, organic or other readily oxidizable material (paper, wood, sulfur, aluminum or plastics).
	Conditions to avoid:
	Heat
Potassium ferro cyanide	Metal chlorates, perchlorates, nitrates, or nitrites may cause violent explosions. May liberate toxic cyanide fumes when mixed with strong acids.

(*Continued*)

Table 4.2 (Continued) Chemical Incompatibilities

Chemical	Incompatibilities
Potassium hydroxide	Contact with water, acids, flammable liquids and organic halogen compounds, especially trichloroethylene, may cause fire or explosion. Contact with nitromethane and other similar nitro compounds cause formation of shock sensitive salts. Contact with metals such as aluminum, tin, and zinc causes formation of flammable hydrogen gas.
	Conditions to avoid:
	Heat, moisture
Potassium nitrate	Heavy metals, phosphites, organic compounds, carbonaceous materials, strong acids, and many other substances
	Conditions to avoid:
	Heat, flames, ignition sources
Potassium perchlorate	Aluminum, magnesium, charcoal, fluorine, sulfur, many combustible substances and reducing agents
	Conditions to avoid:
	Heat, flames, ignition sources
Potassium permanganate	Powdered metals, alcohol, arsenites, bromides, iodides, phosphorous, sulfuric acid, organic compounds, sulfur, activated carbon, hydrides, strong hydrogen peroxide, ferrous or mercurous salts, hypophosphites, hyposulfites, sulfites, peroxides, and oxalates
	Conditions to avoid:
	Heat, flames, ignition sources
Powdered tin	N/A
Propylene chlorohydrin	Strong oxidizing agents, strong acids, acid chlorides, acid anhydrides
	Conditions to avoid:
	Ignition sources, excess heat
Pyridine	Strong oxidizers, strong acids
3-Pyridol	Strong oxidizing agents, strong acids and bases
Pyrolidine	N/A
Rhombic sulfur	N/A
Silica gel	Diazomethane, aluminum, phosphorous. Reacts with hydrogen fluoride, strong acids, and strong bases.
	Conditions to avoid:
	Air, moisture
Silver nitrate	Ammonia, alkalis, antimony salts, arsenites, bromides, carbonates, chlorides, iodides, thiocyanates, ferrous salts, phosphates, tannic acid, and tartrates.
	Conditions to avoid:
	Heat, flame, sources of ignition, light

Table 4.2 (Continued) Chemical Incompatibilities

Chemical	Incompatibilities
Sodium	Water, oxygen, carbon dioxide, carbon tetrachloride, halogens, acetylene, metal halides, ammonium salts, oxides, oxidizing agents, acids, alcohols, chlorinated organic compounds, many other substances. **Conditions to avoid:** Air, heat, flames, ignition sources
Sodium acetate	Nitric acid, fluoride, potassium nitrate, strong oxidizers, and diketene
Sodium azide	Benzoyl chloride plus potassium hydroxide, bromine, carbon disulfide, chromyl chloride, copper, dibromalononitrile, dimethyl sulfate, lead, barium carbonate, sulfuric acid, water, and nitric acid **Conditions to avoid:** Heat, flames, ignition sources
Sodium bicarbonate	Reacts with acids to form carbon dioxide. Dangerous reaction with monoammonium phosphate or a sodium-potassium alloy. **Conditions to avoid:** Heat, moisture
Sodium bisulfate	Water, acids, alkalis, sodium nitrite, oxidizers, aluminum powder **Conditions to avoid:** Moisture, heat, flames, ignition sources
Sodium carbonate	Fluorine, aluminum, phosphorous pentoxide, sulfuric acid, zinc, lithium, moisture, calcium hydroxide and 2,4,6-trinitrotoluene. Reacts violently with acids to form carbon dioxide. **Conditions to avoid:** Moisture, heat, dusting
Sodium chlorate	Aluminum, strong acids, strong reducing agents, organic matter and other oxidizable substances. **Conditions to avoid:** Heat, flame, ignition sources, shock, friction
Sodium chloride	Lithium, bromine trifluoride
Sodium cyanide	Acid, nitrates, nitrites, chlorates, fluorine, magnesium, and strong oxidizers. Reacts with acids to liberate toxic and flammable hydrogen cyanide gas. Water or weak alkaline solutions can produce dangerous amounts of hydrogen cyanide in confined areas. Reacts with carbon dioxide in air to form hydrogen cyanide gas. **Conditions to avoid:** Heat, moisture
Sodium ferro cyanide	N/A

(Continued)

Table 4.2 (Continued) Chemical Incompatibilities

Chemical	Incompatibilities
Sodium fluoride	Reacts with acids to form hydrogen fluoride.
Sodium hydroxide	Sodium hydroxide in contact with acids and organic halogen compounds, especially trichloroethylene, may causes violent reactions. Contact with nitromethane and other similar nitro compounds cause formation of shock-sensitive salts. Contact with metals such as aluminum, magnesium, tin, and zinc cause formation of flammable hydrogen gas. Sodium hydroxide, even in fairly dilute solution, reacts readily with various sugars to produce carbon monoxide. Precautions should be taken including monitoring the tank atmosphere for carbon monoxide to ensure safety of personnel before vessel entry.
	Conditions to avoid:
	Moisture, dusting
Sodium peroxide	Moisture, organic and oxidizable substances, acetic acid, acetic anhydride, aluminum, aluminum plus carbon dioxide, ammonium persulfate, aniline, antimony, arsenic, benzene, boron nitride, calcium carbide, charcoal, dextrose plus potassium nitrate, diethyl ether, glycerine, hexamethylenetetramine, hydrogen sulfide, magnesium, magnesium plus carbon dioxide, manganese dioxide, organic matter, phosphorus, potassium selenium monochloride, silver chloride plus charcoal, sodium, sulfur monochloride, tin, and zinc, reducing agents.
	Conditions to avoid:
	Heat, flames, ignition sources
Sodium sulfide monohydrate	N/A
Sodium sulfate	In combination with sodium sulfate, aluminum, and magnesium will explode at 800°C (1472°F); strong mineral acids and bases.
	Conditions to avoid:
	Air
Starch	Strong oxidizers
	Conditions to avoid:
	Heat, flames, ignition sources
Strontium nitrate	Reducing agents, organic compounds, halogens
	Conditions to avoid:
	Heat, flames, ignition sources
Sulfur	Chlorates, nitrates, and other oxidizing agents. Halogens, carbides, zinc, tin, alkali metals, phosphorus, ammonia, ammonium nitrate, charcoal, and many other substances
	Conditions to avoid:
	Heat, flame, ignition sources, dusting

Table 4.2 (Continued) Chemical Incompatibilities

Chemical	Incompatibilities
Sulfur trioxide	Organic materials, finely powdered metals, bases, water, cyanides, and a wide variety of other chemicals. Reacts violently with water and oxygen. **Conditions to avoid:** Excess heat, exposure to moist air or water, freezing temperatures, confined spaces
Sulfuric acid	Water, potassium chlorate, potassium perchlorate, potassium permanganate, sodium, lithium, bases, organic material, halogens, metal acetylides, oxides and hydrides, metals (yields hydrogen gas), strong oxidizing and reducing agents, and many other reactive substances **Conditions to Avoid:** Heat, moisture
Tetraethyl lead	N/A
Tetrahydrofuran	Tetrahydrofuran reacts violently with air on standing. $LiAlH_2$, strong oxidizers, $NaAlH_2$, and potassium hydroxide. Will attack some forms of plastics, rubbers, and coatings. **Conditions to avoid:** Heat, flame, ignition sources, light, and air
Thionyl chloride	Water, ammonia, chloryl perchlorate, dimethyl sulfoxide, linseed oil, quinoline, sodium, 2,4-hexadiyn-1-6-diol, o-nitrobenzoyl acetic acid, and o-nitrophenylacetic acid **Conditions to avoid:** Heat, moisture
Thiophosphorus trichloride	N/A
Trimethylamine	Bases, acids, oxidizing agents, brass, zinc, magnesium, aluminum, mercury, mercury oxides, acid chlorides, and acid anhydrides
Thorium nitrate	Strong oxidizers
Toluene	Heat, flame, strong oxidizers, nitric and sulfuric acids, chlorine, nitrogen tetraoxide; will attack some forms of plastics, rubber, coatings. **Conditions to avoid:** Heat, flames, ignition sources
Tributanolamine	N/A
Triethanolamine	Copper, copper alloys, galvanized iron, acids, and oxidizers **Conditions to avoid:** Heat, ignition sources, moisture
Xylene	Strong oxidizing agents and strong acids **Conditions to avoid:** Heat, flames, ignition sources

(Continued)

Table 4.2 (Continued) Chemical Incompatibilities

Chemical	Incompatibilities
Zinc (powder)	Zinc powder can react violently with water, sulfur, and halogens. Dangerous or potentially dangerous with strong oxidizing agents, lower molecular weight chlorinated hydrocarbons, strong acids and alkalis. **Conditions to avoid:** Heat, flames, ignition sources

Chemical Compatibility

Table 4.3 Dangerous Goods and Combustible Liquids Storage

Class or Subsidiary Risk	2	2	TOXIC GAS 2	2	3	4	4	4	5.1	5.2	TOXIC 6	CORROSIVE 8
FLAMMABLE GASES	OK TO STORE TOGETHER	OK TO STORE TOGETHER	SEGREGATE At least 3m	SEGREGATE At least 3m	SEGREGATE At least 5m	SEGREGATE At least 5m	SEGREGATE At least 5m	SEGREGATE At least 5m	SEGREGATE At least 3m	ISOLATE	SEGREGATE At least 3m	SEGREGATE At least 5m
NON TOXIC NON FLAMMABLE GASES	OK TO STORE TOGETHER	OK TO STORE TOGETHER	OK TO STORE TOGETHER	OK TO STORE TOGETHER	SEGREGATE At least 5m	SEGREGATE At least 5m	SEGREGATE At least 5m	SEGREGATE At least 5m	SEGREGATE At least 3m	ISOLATE	SEGREGATE At least 3m	SEGREGATE At least 5m
TOXIC GAS	SEGREGATE At least 3m	OK TO STORE TOGETHER	MAY NOT BE COMPATIBLE CHECK MSDS AND NOTES	SEGREGATE At least 3m	SEGREGATE At least 5m	SEGREGATE At least 5m	SEGREGATE At least 5m	SEGREGATE At least 5m	SEGREGATE At least 3m	ISOLATE	SEGREGATE At least 3m	SEGREGATE At least 5m
OXIDIZING GAS	SEGREGATE At least 3m	OK TO STORE TOGETHER	SEGREGATE At least 3m	OK TO STORE TOGETHER	SEGREGATE At least 5m	SEGREGATE At least 5m	SEGREGATE At least 5m	SEGREGATE At least 5m	SEGREGATE At least 3m	ISOLATE	SEGREGATE At least 3m	SEGREGATE At least 5m
FLAMMABLE LIQUIDS + COMBUSTIBLE LIQUIDS	SEGREGATE At least 5m	SEGREGATE At least 5m	SEGREGATE At least 5m	SEGREGATE At least 5m	OK TO STORE TOGETHER	SEGREGATE At least 3m	SEGREGATE At least 5m	SEGREGATE At least 5m	SEGREGATE At least 5m	ISOLATE	SEGREGATE At least 5m	SEGREGATE At least 3m
FLAMMABLE SOLID	SEGREGATE At least 5m	SEGREGATE At least 5m	SEGREGATE At least 5m	SEGREGATE At least 5m	SEGREGATE At least 3m	OK TO STORE TOGETHER	SEGREGATE At least 3m	SEGREGATE At least 5m	SEGREGATE At least 3m	ISOLATE	SEGREGATE At least 3m	MAY NOT BE COMPATIBLE CHECK MSDS AND NOTES
SPONTANEOUSLY COMBUSTIBLE	SEGREGATE At least 5m	SEGREGATE At least 5m	SEGREGATE At least 5m	SEGREGATE At least 5m	SEGREGATE At least 5m	SEGREGATE At least 3m	OK TO STORE TOGETHER	SEGREGATE At least 5m	SEGREGATE At least 5m	ISOLATE	SEGREGATE At least 3m	SEGREGATE At least 3m
DANGEROUS WHEN WET	SEGREGATE At least 5m	SEGREGATE At least 5m	SEGREGATE At least 5m	SEGREGATE At least 5m	SEGREGATE At least 5m	SEGREGATE At least 5m	SEGREGATE At least 5m	OK TO STORE TOGETHER	SEGREGATE At least 5m	ISOLATE	SEGREGATE At least 3m	SEGREGATE At least 5m
OXIDIZING AGENT	SEGREGATE At least 3m	SEGREGATE At least 3m	SEGREGATE At least 3m	SEGREGATE At least 3m	SEGREGATE At least 5m	KEEP APART	SEGREGATE At least 5m	SEGREGATE At least 5m	MAY NOT BE COMPATIBLE CHECK MSDS AND NOTES	ISOLATE	SEGREGATE At least 3m	SEGREGATE At least 3m
ORGANIC PEROXIDE	ISOLATE	ISOLATE	ISOLATE	ISOLATE	ISOLATE	ISOLATE	ISOLATE	ISOLATE	ISOLATE	OK TO STORE TOGETHER	ISOLATE	SEGREGATE At least 3m
TOXIC SUBSTANCES	SEGREGATE At least 3m	SEGREGATE At least 3m	SEGREGATE At least 3m	SEGREGATE At least 3m	SEGREGATE At least 5m	SEGREGATE At least 3m	SEGREGATE At least 3m	SEGREGATE At least 3m	SEGREGATE At least 3m	ISOLATE	OK TO STORE TOGETHER	SEGREGATE At least 5m
CORROSIVE	SEGREGATE At least 5m	SEGREGATE At least 5m	SEGREGATE At least 5m	SEGREGATE At least 5m	SEGREGATE At least 3m	MAY NOT BE COMPATIBLE CHECK MSDS AND NOTES	SEGREGATE At least 3m	SEGREGATE At least 5m	SEGREGATE At least 3m	SEGREGATE At least 3m	SEGREGATE At least 5m	MAY NOT BE COMPATIBLE CHECK MSDS AND NOTES

Color	Material Class	HCC	Yellow B1-B3	Light Blue C1,C3	Blue C2	Purple C4	Light Gray D1,D2	Gray D3	Tan D4	Red F1-F4, F8	Pink F5,F6	Orange F7	Light Green N1	Black T1,T4-T7	Green V2-V7
Yellow	Corrosive Alkali	B1-B3	B1-B3	o	o	x	x	x	x	o	o	o	o	o	+
Light Blue	Corrosive Acid, Inorganic	C1,C3	o	C1,C3	o	o	x	o	x	o	o	o	o	o	o
Blue	Corrosive Acid, Organic	C2	o	o	C2	x	x	x	x	o	o	o	x	o	+
Purple	Acid, Corrosive and Oxidizer, Inorganic	C4	x	o	x	C4	o	x	x	x	o	x	x	o	o
Light Gray	Oxidizer/Oxidizer and Poison	D1,D2	x	x	x	o	D1,D2	o	o	x	x	x	o	o	x
Gray	Oxidizer and Corrosive, Acidic	D3	x	o	x	x	o	D3	o	x	x	x	x	o	o
Tan	Oxidizer and Corrosive, Alkali	D4	x	x	x	x	o	o	D4	x	x	x	x	o	o
Red	Flammable Liquids and Solids	F1-F4, F8	o	o	o	x	x	x	x	F1-F4, F8	o	o	o	o	o
Pink	Flammable Liquids, Poison and Acidic	F5,F6	o	o	o	o	x	x	x	o	F5,F6	o	o	+	o
Orange	Flammable Liquid and Corrosive, Alkali	F7	o	o	o	x	x	x	x	o	o	F7	o	o	o
Light Green	Not Regulated as Hazardous	N1	o	o	x	x	o	x	x	o	o	o	N1	o	+
Black	Toxics/Poisons	T1,T4-T7	o	o	o	o	o	o	o	o	+	o	o	T1, T4-T7	+
Green	Aerosols and/or Petroleum Products	V2-V7	+	o	+	o	x	o	o	o	o	o	+	+	V2-V7

Key

x	Prohibited - Cannot be stored in the same compartment unless segregated by a NAVSEA approved cabinet
o	Restricted - Separated in a manner that, in the event of leakage, mixing of hazardous materials would not occur
+	Allowed - Storage together is authorized

Notes:

(1) Solids shall be stored above liquids

(2) Follow the HCC process for obtaining missing or incorrect HCCs (CHRIMP Technician Deskguide)

(3) For items not covered by the above matrix, consult HM coordinator, CHRIMP Technician, or NSTM 670 Appendix E

HCC-Specific Guidance:

(1) C1-C4: Store concentrated nitric acid in acid locker, and keep distance from other acids. Store Bromine Cartridges in dedicated cabinets.

(2) D4: Store Calcium Hypochorite in designated NAVSEA approved locker. Do not store oxidizers in same compartment with flammables or combustibles.

(3) G1-G9: Mount all stored gas cylinders to prevent them from falling or rolling (Grade B shock). Keep maximum distance possible between flammable (G2, G8) and oxidizer (G4, G7, G9) gases when not in use (e.g., oxygen/acetylene in welding)

(4) V2, V3: All aerosols will be stored together within the same location within a storeroom. Further segregate aerosols from flammable liquids and gases in the same space using wire mesh or other barrier (e.g., locker) to prevent projectiles in case of fire

Figure 4.5 Chemical Compatibility Matrix.

Site Control

5

A First Responder's Guide

First Responders Who Encounter a Suspected Clandestine Lab Should:

- Not touch anything
  - Boobie traps are common
  - Chemicals or reactions mixtures may be unstable
  - Unknown chemicals create unknown hazards
- Removal everyone from the immediate area
  - Distance will be determined by the type of lab encountered
- Establish a secure perimeter
  - Distance will be determined by the type of lab encountered
  - See pages 75–78 for guidance
- Notify proper authorities
  - Law Enforcement
    - Local clandestine drug lab team
    - Local bomb squad
  - Local Fire Department
  - Hazardous Materials Team
- Wait until trained personnel arrive

Observation Guide

Cap Color	Acid
Blue	Hydrochloric Acid (HCl)
Yellow	Sulfuric Acid (H_2SO_4)
Brown	Acetic Acid (CH_3COOH)
Red	Nitric Acid (HNO_3)
Clear/White	Phosphoric Acid (H_3PO_4)
Black	Perchloric Acid ($HClO_4$)
Black	Hydriodic Acid (HI)

Figure 5.1 Acid Cap Color Code.

DOI: 10.4324/9781003335139-5

Priority of Hazards

1. Flammable/Explosive atmospheres
2. Toxic atmosphere
3. Damaged or leaking cylinders
4. Sources of ignition
5. Incompatible chemicals
6. Boobie traps
7. Reactions in progress
8. Confined spaces
9. Unstable chemical storage
10. Pressurized containers
11. Unknown chemicals

Table 5.1 Noting Site and Lab Conditions

Site Conditions	Lab Conditions	Chemical
• Difficult or limited entry/exit • Poor ventilation • Poor visibility or lighting • Limited work area • Debris/obstacles/clutter • Visible contamination • Fire/explosion damage • Underground/confined space • Uneven/unsupported walking surface • Electrical wiring	• Boxed or operational • # of containers • Condition of containers • Glassware (scientific v. household) • Glassware (condition) • Chemical storage	• List all visible labels • Container labels (labeled v. unlabeled) • Container labels (factory v. handwritten) • Color, appearance of unlabeled chemicals • Volume/quantity • Multi-layer liquids

BOMB THREAT STAND-OFF CHART

Threat Description Improvised Explosive Device (IED)	Explosives Capacity[1] (TNT Equivalent)	Building Evacuation Distance[2]	Outdoor Evacuation Distance[3]
Pipe Bomb	5 LBS	70 FT	1200 FT
Suicide Bomber	20 LBS	110 FT	1700 FT
Briefcase/Suitcase	50 LBS	150 FT	1850 FT
Car	500 LBS	320 FT	1500 FT
SUV/Van	1,000 LBS	400 FT	2400 FT
Small Moving Van/ Delivery Truck	4,000 LBS	640 FT	3800 FT
Moving Van/ Water Truck	10,000 LBS	860 FT	5100 FT
Semi-Trailer	60,000 LBS	1570 FT	9300 FT

1. These capacities are based on the maximum weight of explosive material that could reasonably fit in a container of similar size.
2. Personnel in buildings are provided a high degree of protection from death or serious injury; however, glass breakage and building debris may still cause some injuries. Unstrengthened buildings can be expected to sustain damage that approximates five percent of their replacement cost.
3. If personnel cannot enter a building to seek shelter they must evacuate to the minimum distance recommended by Outdoor Evacuation Distance. These distance is governed by the greater hazard of fragmentation distance, glass breakage or threshold for ear drum rupture.

Figure 5.2 Blast Setback Distances.

Source: DHS.

It is important to note that the given distances do not guarantee safety, they are estimates based on test data and the area near and around the evacuation distances are still potentially dangerous. Minimum evacuation distance is the range at which a life-threatening injury from blast or fragmentation hazards is unlikely. However, non-life-threatening injury or temporary hearing loss may occur.

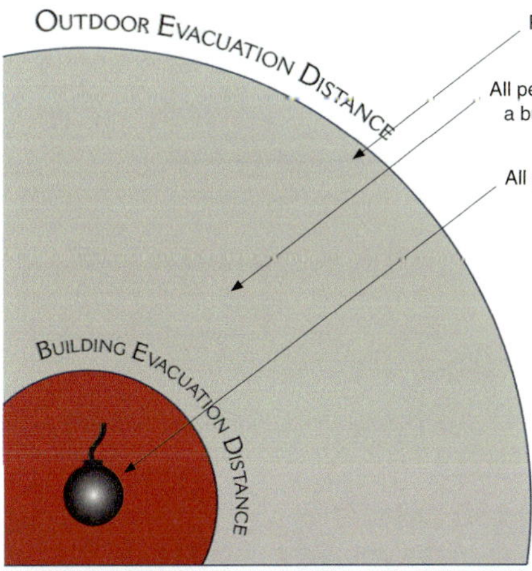

Preferred area (beyond this line) for evacuation of people in buildings and mandatory for people outdoors.

All personnel in this area should seek shelter immediately inside a building away from windows and exterior walls. Avoid having anyone outside - including those evacuating - in this area.

All personnel must evacuate (both inside of buildings and out).

1. Based on maximum volume or weight of explosive (TNT equivalent) that could reasonably fit in a suitcase or vehicle.
2. Governed by the ability of typical US commercial construction to resist severe damage or collapse following a blast. Performance can vary significantly, however, and buildings should be analyzed by qualified parties when possible.
3. Governed by the greater of fragment throw distance or glass breakage/falling glass hazard distance. Note that pipe and briefcase bombs assume cased charges that throw fragments farther than vehicle bombs.
4. A known terrorist tactic is to attract bystanders to windows, doorways, and the outside with gunfire, small bombs, or other methods and then detonate a larger, more destructive device, significantly increasing human casualties.

Figure 5.3 Outdoor Evacuation Distances.

Source: DHS.

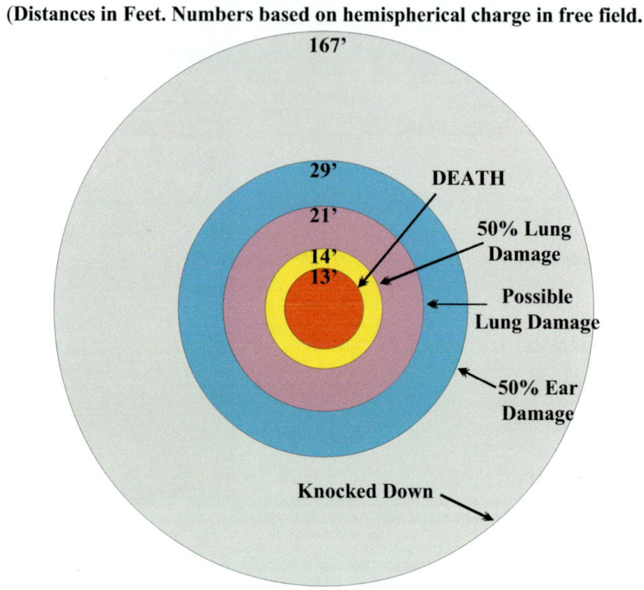

TNT	1 psi	15 psi	30 psi	75 psi	100 psi
1 lb.	46	8	6	4	3.4
10 lb.	98	17	13	8.4	7.4
50 lb.	167	29	21	14	13
500 lb.	360	63	46	31	27
5000 lb.	775	136	99	66	59

Figure 5.4 Blast Effects.

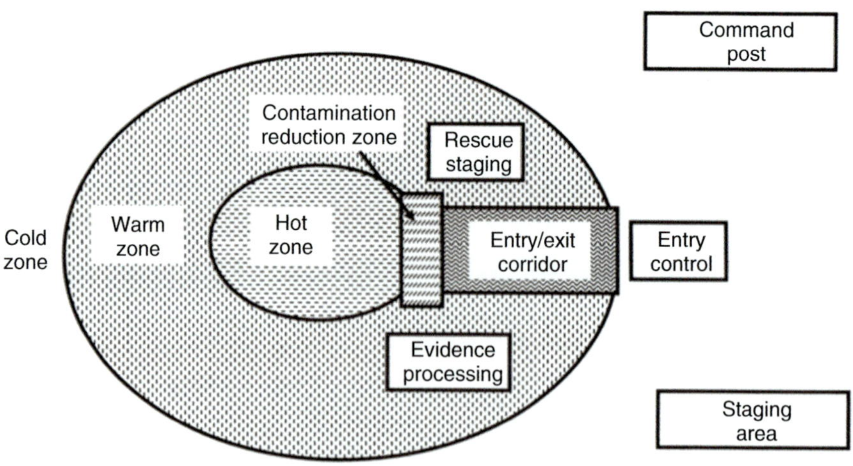

Figure 5.5 Site Control Diagram.

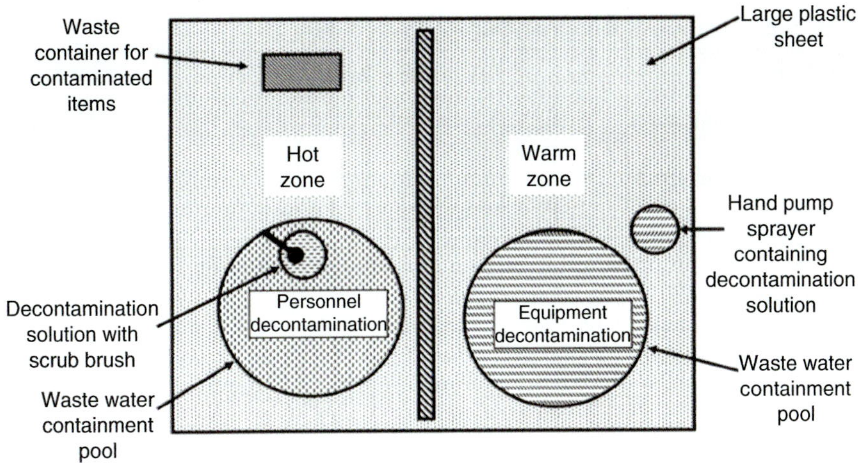

Figure 5.6 Contamination Reduction Zone.

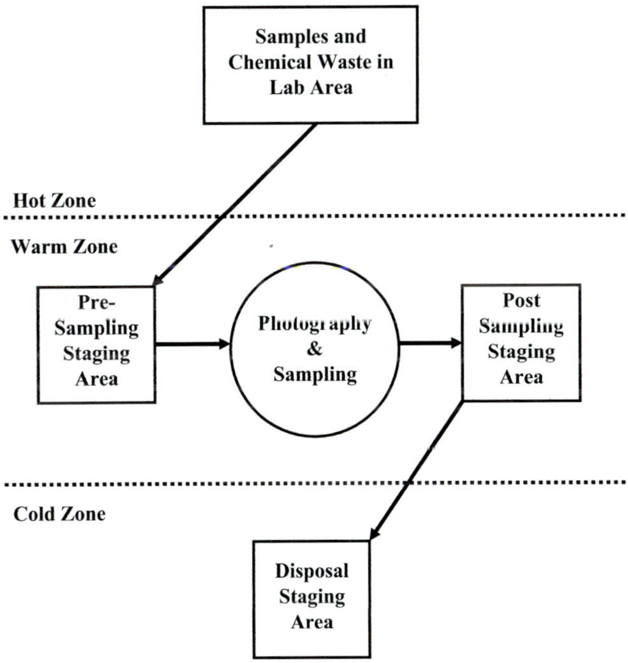

Figure 5.7 Sample/Waste Flow.

Table 5.2 Maximum Decontamination Procedures

Hot Zone	Warm Zone	Cold Zone
1. Segregated equipment drop	7. Suit and boot wash	18. Field wash
2. Boot cover and glove wash	8. Suit and boot rinse	19. Redress
3. Boot cover and glove rinse	9. Tank change and reentry (levels A and B) OR cartridge change and reentry (level C)	
4. Tape removal	10. Boot removal	
5. Boot cover removal	11. Suit removal (levels A and C) OR tank removal (level B)	
6. Outer glove removal	12. Tank backpack removal (level A) OR suit removal (level B)	
	13. Inner glove wash	
	14. Inner glove rinse	
	15. Face mask removal	
	16. Inner glove removal	
	17. Inner clothing removal	

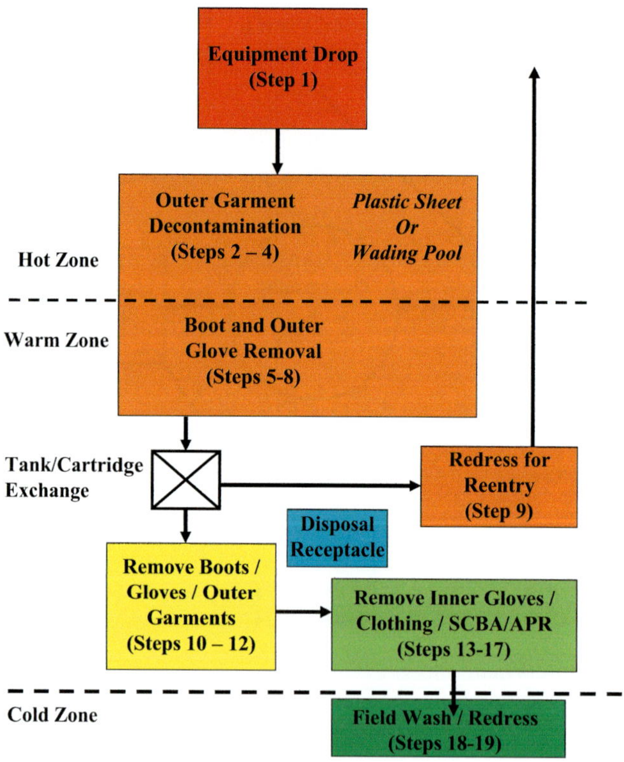

Figure 5.8 Decontamination Site Diagram.

Table 5.3 Decontamination Solutions

Solution A: For inorganic acids, heavy metals, etc.	• 1 gallon water • 6.5 oz (by weight) sodium carbonate • 6.5 oz (by weight) trisodium phosphate (TSP)
Solution B: For chlorinated phenols and oils, cyanides, ammonia, and other non-acidic inorganic wastes	• 1 gallon water • 13 oz (by weight) calcium hypochlorite
Solution C (General use): For oil, grease, solvents, organic compounds, and unspecified substances	• 1 gallon water • 6.5 oz (by weight) trisodium phosphate
Solution D: For inorganic bases, alkali and caustic substances	• 1 gallon water • 1.5 fluid oz concentrated hydrochloric acid (muratic acid)

Table 5.4 Emergency Exposure Procedure

Chemical Exposure	Emergency Decontamination
• Move to safe location • Remove contaminated clothing • Flush exposed skin with large volume of water • Seek medical help	• Bypass the decon station • Move to safe location • Stand in a large open garbage bag • Remove and drop all PPE into the garbage bag • Step out of and seal garbage bag • Wash face and hands with disposable wipes or a cloth and water

Table 5.5 Chemical Exposure First Aid Procedures

Inhalation	Ingestion	Dermal Exposure
• Move to fresh air • Loosen clothing • Maintain air way • Avoid movement • Clear particulates from nasal airway • Make victim comfortable • Treat for shock • Call of assistance • Monitor respiration and pulse	• Remove from contaminated area • If conscious, rinse mouth with water • DO NOT INDUCE VOMITING • Loosen clothing • Make victim comfortable • Prevent aspiration of vomit • Treat for shock • Call of assistance • Monitor respiration and pulse	• Remove from contaminated area • Remove contaminated clothing • Flush with water for 15–30 minutes (face first) • Make victim comfortable • Treat for shock • Call of assistance • Monitor respiration and pulse

Table 5.6 EPA PPE Selection Guidelines

Respiratory Protection	Protective Clothing	Hand and Foot Protection	Optional Equipment Level A
		Level A	
• NIOSH approved positive pressure full face piece SCBA, or • NIOSH approved positive pressure full face piece supplied air respirator with an EEBA (5-minute duration minimum)	• Totally encapsulated chemical protective suit specifically designed to resist penetration by chemicals that are encountered.	• Gloves: outer and inner chemical- resistant gloves • Boots: Chemical- resistant with steel toe and shank	• Coveralls • Long underwear • Hard hat • 2-way radio communication system
		Level B	
• NIOSH approved positive pressure full face piece SCBA, or • NIOSH approved positive pressure full face piece supplied air respirator with an EEBA (5-minute duration minimum)	• Hooded chemical- resistant clothing made of materials resistant to the chemicals encountered (overalls) and long sleeved jacket: coveralls; one or two piece chemical splash suit; disposable chemical resistant overalls.	• Gloves: outer and inner chemical- resistant gloves • Boots: Chemical- resistant with steel toe and shank	• Coveralls • Long underwear • Hard hat • 2-way radio communication system • Face shield • Boot covers (chemical resistant)
		Level C	
• NIOSH-approved full face piece or half mask air purifying respirator	• Hooded chemical- resistant clothing made of materials resistant to the chemicals encountered (overalls) and long sleeved jacket: coveralls; one or two piece chemical splash suit; disposable chemical resistant overalls.	• Gloves: outer and inner chemical- resistant gloves • Boots: Chemical- resistant with steel toe and shank	• Coveralls • Long underwear • Hard hat • 2-way radio communication system • Face shield • Boot covers (chemical resistant) • EEBA
		Level D	
• No respiratory protection required	• Coveralls	• Boots: Chemical- resistant with steel toe and shank	• All the above plus: • Eye/face protection • Gloves

Table 5.7 PPE Issues Glove Selection Guide

Glove Type	Use Type	Advantages	Disadvantages
Nitrile, Disposable	• Incidental chemical contact use only • General lab chemical use • Commonly used in the medical field	• Good general lab use glove, adequate protection from many organic solvents, oils, greases, and some acids and bases • Good protection from blood, cell lines, and tissue • Clear indication of tears and breaks • Excellent dexterity • Non-allergenic	• Not effective for direct contact use • Not effective for use with many halogenated solvents
Neoprene, Disposable	• Incidental chemical contact use only • General lab chemical use	• Good protection from many acids, bases, peroxides, fuels, alcohols, and phenols • Clear indication of tears and breaks • Excellent dexterity	• Not effective for direct contact use • Not effective for use with many halogenated solvents
Latex, Disposable	• Incidental chemical contact use only • Commonly used in the medical field • Not suitable for many lab settings	• Good protection from many biological agents, including blood, cell lines, and tissue • Provides good protection from some acids and bases • Excellent dexterity	• Not effective for direct contact use • Not effective for use with many organic solvents • Allergenic • Difficult to detect tears and breaks
Butyl Rubber	• Suitable for direct contact with some chemicals	• Good protection from many ketones, esters, gases, vapors, acids, and bases • Can be decontaminated reused • Puncture and tear resistant	• Not effective for use with gasoline, aliphatic, aromatic, and halogenated hydrocarbons • Poor dexterity

(*Continued*)

Table 5.7 (Continued) PPE Issues Glove Selection Guide

Glove Type	Use Type	Advantages	Disadvantages
Viton	• Suitable for direct contact with some chemicals	• Good protection from many chlorinated and aromatic hydrocarbons • Can be decontaminated reused • Puncture and tear resistant	• Not effective for use with ketones • Average dexterity
Polyvinyl Chloride	• Suitable for direct contact with some chemicals	• Good protection from many acids, bases, oils, fats, peroxides, and amines • Can be decontaminated reused • Puncture and tear resistant	• Not effective for use with many organic solvents • Average dexterity

https://www.purdue.edu/ehps/rem/laboratory/Personal/PPE/gloveselection.pdf

Scene Processing

6

Table 6.1 Initial Assessment Guide

Do	Don't
• Identify flammable, explosive, toxic chemical atmospheres • Identify potential booby traps • Isolate ignition sources • Identify active chemical reactions • Identify reaction type and location • Identify chemicals and incompatible combinations • Identify chemical storage location, conditions, and quantities • Close open containers • Identify equipment (scientific v. household) • Identify fire or explosion damage • Properly ventilate confined spaces • Identify possible electrical hazards • Identify all slip, trip, and fall hazards • Identify unsafe all other unsafe working conditions • Identify all points of entry and exit • Report observations to site safety officer for abatement plan development	• Do not enter the lab scene without proper training. • Do not process the lab scene unless all qualified personnel are present. • Do not enter the lab scene without the appropriate safety equipment. • Do not handle chemicals unless trained. • Do not handle booby traps unless properly trained. • Do not handle active chemical. reactions unless absolutely necessary. • Do not perform field tests unless properly trained. • Do not handle compressed gas containers unless absolutely necessary. • Do not perform hazard abatement procedures until consulting with site safety officer.

DOI: 10.4324/9781003335139-6

EMERGENCY REACTION SHUTDOWN GUIDE

WARNING: DO NOT ATTEMPT THIS UNLESS YOU HAVE BEEN TRAINED IN THE CLANDESTINE MANUFACTURE OF DRUGS OR EXPLOSIVES.

- Determine whether the reaction is being heated, cooled, or both.
- Remove heat from the reaction vessel.
- Maintain cooling to the reaction until the reaction appears to have gone to completion and the vessel is cool to the touch.
- Remove obstructions and ventilation tubing from the top of condensing columns.
  - Cooling reactions can create a vacuum that could hamper the dismantling of the apparatus.
  - If the reaction is being vented into water the vacuum created by the cooling reaction could draw the water into the hot reaction mixture leading to a violent reaction.
- If necessary, compressed gas containers connected to a reaction vessel should be turned off at the source.
  - The pressure of the reaction vessel should be allowed to naturally reduce to atmospheric pressure.
  - Release of pressurized contents of the reaction vessel may create a toxic exposure.
- Systems under vacuum should be slowly brought back to atmospheric pressure.
  - Water or oxygen in the air may react violently with the chemicals in vessel under vacuum.
- Filtration processes should be allowed to naturally go to completion.

Table 6.2 Hazardous Materials Handling Guidelines

Explosive Chemicals 	• Do not handle chemicals unless trained or absolutely necessary. • The handling of chemicals should be left to trained personnel. Trained personnel can recognize chemical names that have explosive potential. They also can recognize chemical combinations or other situations with explosive potential. Untrained personnel should seal the area of the clandestine lab and wait for trained personnel to affect the abatement procedures. • Separate incompatible chemicals. Trained personnel should separate chemicals with known incompatibility. This will reduce the potential for these chemicals to accidentally combine and create an explosive situation.

Table 6.2 (Continued) Hazardous Materials Handling Guidelines

	• Remove heat from reaction mixtures. This will slow or stop the reaction that is taking place. This will reduce the amount of potentially explosive and toxic fumes that are being produced. Allowing the reaction mixture to reduce to room temperature naturally eliminates the effect of drastic changes in temperature. • Ventilate confined spaces. This will reduce the concentration of explosive fumes in the area to below the explosive limit. • Do not open valves. • Close valves of containers connected to reaction apparatus. • Secure container for chemical disposal company disposal.
Flammable/Combustible 	• Do not handle chemicals unless trained or absolutely necessary. • Separate incompatible chemicals. • Remove heat from reaction mixtures. • Ventilate confined spaces. • Isolate from ignition source. All fire needs fuel, oxygen, and a source of ignition. Removing the source of ignition removes the capacity to burn. (The muzzle flash from a discharged weapon is sufficient to ignite a flammable atmosphere.)
Acids and Caustics 	• Do not handle chemicals unless trained or absolutely necessary. • Identify the pH and/or acid type of all unknown liquids. Knowing the basic characteristics of the liquids will provide insight into how they should be segregated. (See Table 2.1 for bottle cap identification guide.) • Seal all containers. This reduces the likelihood of the mixture of liquids if the containers are spilled. Also some mineral acids produce fumes that can contaminate the air or mix with uncovered solutions containing incompatible mixtures. • Separate acids and caustics. Segregating liquids by pH will prevent violent reactions if a chemical spill does occur. • Separated acids by type. All acids are not created equal. Oxidizing mineral acids react violently when they come in contact with non-oxidizing mineral acids and organic acids. Segregating acids by type will prevent violent reactions if a chemical spill does occur.

(*Continued*)

Table 6.2 (Continued) Hazardous Materials Handling Guidelines

Oxidizers and Reducers 	• Do not handle chemicals unless trained or absolutely necessary. • Identify known chemicals form container label. Unfortunately, there is no screening test for the rapid identification of oxidizers or reducers commonly used in the field by chemists investigating clandestine labs in the field. Unlabeled containers should be treated as unknowns leaving the field identification to the chemical waste disposal company. • Seal all containers. This reduces the likelihood of the mixture of incompatible chemicals if the containers are spilled. • Separate oxidizers and reducers. Segregating chemicals by class will prevent violent reactions if a chemical spill does occur. Segregating oxidizers from organic material and other combustible material to prevent fire in case of spill.
Compressed Gas 	• Do not handle containers unless trained or absolutely necessary. • Do not handle containers unless absolutely necessary. Safety outweighs the need to identify the contents of the container.

Sampling Guide

General Considerations

- Consult local statutes and case law concerning the type and amount of samples required.
- Sampling should be conducted in a well-ventilated area, preferably away from the lab area.
- All samples should be photographed with the original container.
- Photographs should contain: Case number, Exhibit number, Date, Scale.

What to Sample

- Finished product.
  - Contraband drugs: The entire amount of
  - Explosives: Pea size to sugar cube size amount (<10 gm).
- All reaction mixtures should be sampled.

- Suspected primary explosive reactions should not be sampled.
- Random samples of waste material should be taken.
- Unlabeled chemical containers should be sampled.
- Sampling of reagents and solvents is left to the discretion of the on-scene chemist.
- Each phase of a multiphase liquid should be sampled.
- The sampling of commercially labeled containers is left to the discretion of the on-scene chemist.
    - Factory sealed containers can be assumed to contain what the label reports.
    - Open commercially labeled containers may or may not contain what the label reports.
- The sampling of glassware is left to the discretion of the on-scene chemist.

Sample Packaging

- Liquid samples should be packaged in glass vials with acid-resistant screw cap and placed inside a sealed zip lock plastic bag.
- Solid samples can be placed into a sealed zip lock plastic bag.
- All samples should be placed inside a second sealed zip lock plastic bag.
- The outer sealed zip lock plastic bag should be marked with the appropriate case information.
- Individual items should be placed into a single container filled with an absorbent material for transportation and storage.
- Explosives/explosive mixture samples should be placed into a portable magazine for transportation and storage.

Sampling Kit Items List

Table 6.3 Sampling Kit

Sampling Items
• Camera (35 mm or digital)
• 6 pair, nitrile gloves
• 30, 1–2 oz. Wide Mouth HDPE with screw caps
• 30, 25-ml disposable volumetric pipettes
• 60, 4″ × 6″ zip lock plastic bags
• 3 pipette bulbs
• 100, 3″ × 5″ index cards
• Marking pens
• Tape
• Ruler or tape measure
• Worksheets or note pads

(*Continued*)

Table 6.3 (Continued) Sampling Kit

- 3–5 gal. plastic bucket wit lid
- Portable explosives magazine
- Absorbent material:
- Kitty litter
- Vermiculite
- Diatomaceous earth

Desirable Items

- Chalk or dry erase board with markers
- Scales (1-kg and 100-kg capacity)
- Field test kit
  - pH paper
  - Refillable butane lighter with extended tip
  - Premixed reagents
  - Colorimetric test instrument
  - Raman spectroscopy
  - Infrared spectroscopy

Table 6.4 Field Test Reagents

Reagent	Formulation
Marquis	0.5-ml formaldehyde combined with 30 ml of sulfuric acid (Store in amber glass vial with acid resistant cap.)
Cobalt thiocyanate	5% aqueous solution of cobalt thiocyanate (CoSCN)
Copper sulfate	• (Solution A) 5% aqueous solution of copper sulfate ($CuSO_4$) • (Solution B) saturated aqueous solution of sodium bicarbonate ($NaHCO_3$)
Dinitrobenzene	• (Solution A) 2% solution of m-dinitrobenzene, in reagent alcohol • (Solution B) 5% solution of sodium hydroxide (NaOH)
pDMBA	• (Solution A) 2% solution of p-dimethylaminobenzaldehyde (pDMBA) • (Solution B) Concentrated hydrochloric acid (HCl)
Silver nitrate	5% aqueous solution of silver nitrate ($AgNO_3$)
Barium chloride	5% aqueous solution of barium chloride ($BaCl_2$)
Diphenylamine	• (Solution A) 1% aqueous solution of diphenylamine • (Solution B) Concentrated sulfuric acid (H_2SO_4) (Store in amber glass vial with acid resistant cap.)
Thymol	• (Solution A) 1% aqueous solution of thymol • (Solution B) Concentrated sulfuric acid (H_2SO_4) (Store in amber glass vial with acid resistant cap.)
Nesslers	• Dissolve 5 g of potassium iodide (KI) and 10 gm of mercuric chloride in 50 ml of deionized water • Dissolve 20 g of potassium hydroxide (KOH) in 50 ml of deionized water • Combine solutions
Methanol/Sodium hydroxide	1 N solution of sodium hydroxide (NaOH) in methanol

Table 6.5 Acid Color Test Chart

Acid	$AgNO_3$ Reagent	$AgNO_3$ + HNO_3	$BaCl_2$ Reagent	$BaCl_2$ + HNO_3	Diphenylamine Reagent
Hydrochloric acid (HCl)	White precipitate	Precipitate remains	No reaction	No reaction	No reaction
Hydriodic acid (HI)	Yellow precipitate	Precipitate remains	No reaction	No reaction	No reaction
Sulfuric acid (H_2SO_4)	White precipitate	Precipitate dissolves	White precipitate	Precipitate dissolves	No reaction
Nitric acid (HNO_3)	No reaction	No reaction	No reaction	No reaction	Blue

Table 6.6 Field Test Reactions

Reagent	Color	Indication
Drugs		
Marquis	Orange	Phenethylamines, Phenylacetic acid
	Purple	Opiates, MDA, MDMA
Cobalt thiocyanate	Blue	Cocaine HCl, PCP, Meperidine, Lidocaine
Copper sulfate	Blue	Ephedrine, Psuedo-ephedrine, Lidocaine
Dinitrobenzene	Purple	Phenylacetone (P2P)
pDMBA	Purple	LSD, indoles
Explosives		
Diphenylamine	Blue	NO_3^-, ClO_3^-, ClO_4^-, Nitro-compounds, Oxidizers
Thymol	Green	NO_3^-
	Brown	ClO_3^-
	Red	RDX, HMX
	Blue green	PETN
Sulfuric acid	Yellow orange	ClO_4^-
Aniline sulfate	Blue interface	ClO_3^-
Nessler's	Orange Parcipitate	NH_4^+
Methanol/NaOH	Red to orange	TNT
	Blue to brown	DNT
Vapour pH	Basic	NH_4^+
Pyridine/NaOH	Blue to brown top layer	Sulfur
Silver nitrate	White Parcipitate	Cl^-, CO_3^{-2}, SO_3^{-2}
	Creme Parcipitate	Br^-
	Yellow Parcipitate	I^-, PO_4^{-3}
	Brown Parcipitate	OH^-
	Black Parcipitate	S^-

(Continued)

Table 6.6 (Continued) Field Test Reactions

Reagent	Color	Indication
$+HNO_3$	Parcipitate remains	Cl^-, Br^-, I^-, S^-
	Parcipitate dissolves	CO_3^{-2}, SO_3^{-2}, PO_4^{-3}, OH^-
Barium chloride	White Parcipitate	CO_3^{-2}, SO_4^{-2}, SO_3^{-2}, PO_4^{-3}
$+HNO_3$	Parcipitateremains	SO_4^{-2}
	Parcipitatedissolves	CO_3^{-2}, SO_3^{-2}, PO_4^{-3}

Volume Estimates

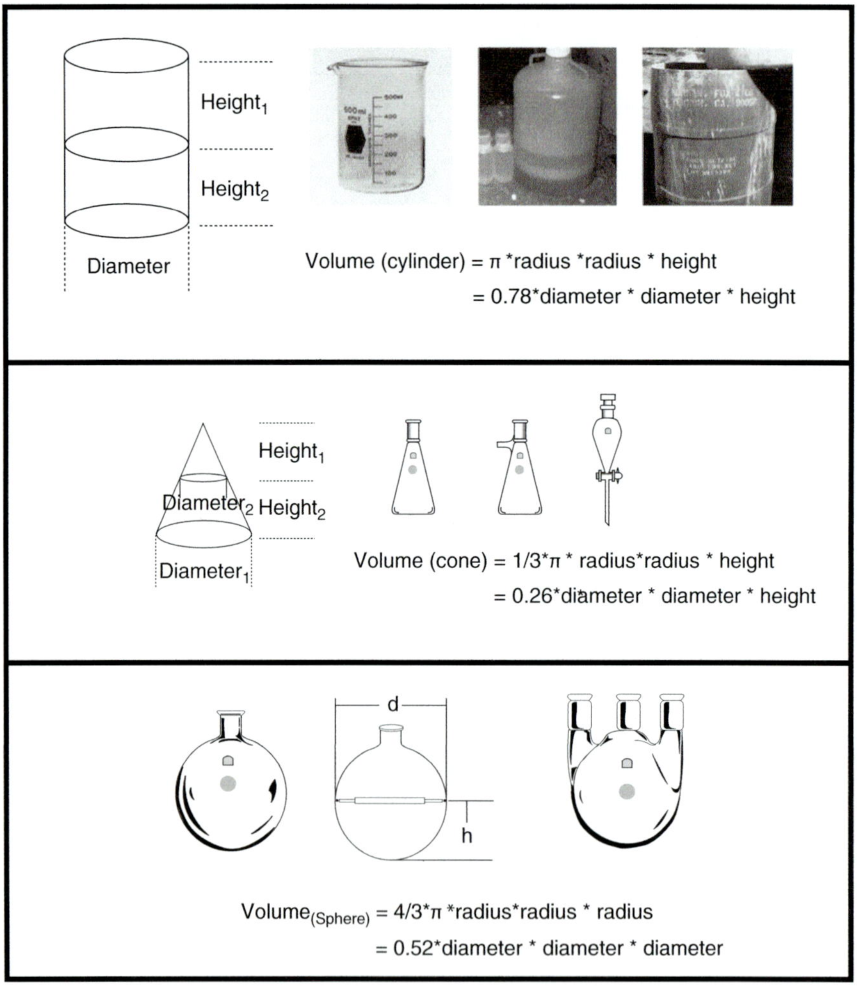

Figure 6.1 Generic Volume Estimates: (a) Cylinder, (b) Cone, (c) Sphere.

Table 6.7 Round Bottom Flask Volume Chart

Liquid Height (cm)	1000 ml	2000 ml	3000 ml	5000 ml	12000 ml	22000 ml	50000 ml	72000 ml
0.5	**5**	**6**	**7**	**9**	**11**	**14**	**18**	**21**
1.0	**19**	**24**	**28**	**33**	**45**	**55**	**73**	**83**
1.5	**42**	**53**	**62**	**74**	**100**	**123**	**163**	**185**
2.0	**79**	**93**	**107**	**129**	**176**	**217**	**288**	**326**
2.5	**109**	**141**	**164**	**198**	**271**	**336**	**447**	**506**
3.0	**152**	**199**	**232**	**280**	**385**	**478**	**638**	**724**
3.5	**200**	**264**	**309**	**348**	**518**	**644**	**862**	**979**
4.0	**252**	**336**	**394**	**481**	**667**	**832**	**1117**	**1270**
4.5	**308**	**414**	**488**	**597**	**833**	**1042**	**1402**	**1596**
5.0	**366**	**497**	**589**	**723**	**1015**	**1273**	**1717**	**1957**
5.5	**426**	**585**	**696**	**859**	**1212**	**1524**	**2061**	**2351**
6.0	**487**	**676**	**808**	**1002**	**1422**	**1794**	**2433**	**2778**
6.5	**549**	**770**	**925**	**153**	**1646**	**2082**	**2832**	**3238**
7.0	**609**	**866**	**1046**	**1310**	**1882**	**2388**	**3258**	**3728**
7.5	**669**	**963**	**1170**	**1473**	**2129**	**2710**	**3709**	**4249**
8.0	**726**	**1061**	**296**	**1641**	**2388**	**3048**	**4185**	**4799**
8.5		**1158**	**1423**	**1812**	**2556**	**3401**	**4685**	**5378**
9.0		**1253**	**1551**	**1987**	**2933**	**3769**	**5208**	**5984**
9.5		**1347**	**1678**	**2165**	**3218**	**4150**	**5753**	**6618**
10.0			**1804**	**2344**	**3510**	**4542**	**6319**	**7278**
10.5			**1929**	**2523**	**3810**	**4948**	**6909**	**7963**
11.0			**2050**	**2703**	**4115**	**5364**	**7513**	**8673**
11.5			**2168**	**2881**	**4424**	**5790**	**8139**	**9407**
12.0			**2281**	**3058**	**4738**	**6225**	**8783**	**10163**
12.5				**3232**	**5055**	**6668**	**9444**	**10942**
13.0				**3402**	**5357**	**7120**	**10121**	**10163**
13.5				**3569**	**5696**	**7577**	**10815**	**12562**
14.0				**3731**	**6017**	**8041**	**11523**	**13402**
14.5					**6340**	**8510**	**12245**	**14261**
15.0					**6661**	**8984**	**12980**	**15137**
15.5					**6980**	**9860**	**13728**	**16031**
16.0					**7297**	**9940**	**14487**	**16941**
16.5					**7610**	**10421**	**15257**	**17867**
17.0					**7920**	**0903**	**16036**	**18807**
17.5					**8224**	**11358**	**16825**	**19761**
18.0					**8522**	**11867**	**17622**	**20729**
18.5						**12347**	**18426**	**21708**
19.0						**12825**	**19237**	**22699**
19.5						**13299**	**20054**	**23700**
20.0						**13771**	**20875**	**24711**

(Continued)

Table 6.7 (Continued) Round Bottom Flask Volume Chart

Liquid Height (cm)	1000 ml	2000 ml	3000 ml	5000 ml	12000 ml	22000 ml	50000 ml	72000 ml
20.5						**14236**	**21701**	**25731**
21.0						**14697**	**22530**	**26758**
21.5							**23361**	**27794**
22.0							**24194**	**28835**
22.5							**25028**	**29882**
23.0							**25862**	**30934**
23.5							**26695**	**31990**
24.0							**27526**	**33049**
24.5							**28354**	**34110**
25.0							**29190**	**35173**
25.5							**30001**	**36236**
26.0							**30817**	**37299**
26.5							**31627**	**38361**
27.0							**32431**	**39421**
27.5								**40479**
28.0								**42533**
28.5								**42583**
29.0								**43627**
29.5								**44666**
30.0								**45967**

Worksheet Guides

7

Date	**Administrative Information**	Case #

Location

Address			City		State
House	Apartment / Hotel	Out Building	Commercial Structure	Rural	Forest / Jungle

Lab Information

Methamphetamine	Amphetamine	PCP	Cocaine	MDA/MDMA	Explosive	Other
Operational			Non Operational		Stored	

Team Assignments

Case Officer		Command Officer	
Site Control		Site Safety	
Chemist		EOD	
Photography		Spokes Person	
Scene Sketch		Evidence Log	
Entry Team	Assessment Team	Search Team	Security Team

Support Services Contact Information

Fire Department	Waste Disposal Company
Ambulance	Hospital
Health Department	Environmental Quality
Child Protective Services	Explosives Disposal

Page _____ of _____

DOI: 10.4324/9781003335139-7

Date	**Hazard Assessment**	Case #

Location

Address	City	State

House	Apartment/ Hotel	Out Building	Commercial Structure	Rural	Forest/ Jungle

Lab Information

Methamphetamine	Amphetamine	PCP	Cocaine	MDA/MDMA	Explosive	Other

Operational	Non Operational	Stored

Hazard Assessment

Hazard Type	**Specific Hazard**	**Location**

Physical Hazards		

PPE Requirements

Zone	**LOCATION**	**A**	**B**	**C**	**D**
Hot					
Warm					
Cold					

Page ______ of ______

Date	**Scene Sketch**	Case #
Location		
Investigator/Chemist		

Sketch

Legend

Page ______ of ______

Date	**Evidence Log**	Case #
Location		
Investigator/Chemist		

Ex. #	**Sampled Y/N**	**Photo Y/N**	**Disposed Y/N**	**Description**

Page ______ of ______

Date	**Non Chemical Inventory**	Case #
Location		
Investigator/Chemist		

Ex. #	**Disposed Y/N**	**Photo Y/N**	**Item Description**	**Total Number**

Page ______ of ______

Date	**Chemical Inventory**	Case #
Location		
Investigator/Chemist		

Ex. #	**Sampled Y/N**	**Description / Label Information (Field Test Results)**	**Estimated Total Amount**

Page ______ of ______

Date	**Top of page**	Case #
Location		
Investigator/Chemist		

PHOTO LOG

Roll #	Photo #	Time	Location	Description

EQUIPMENT/CHEMICAL INVENTORY

Equipment Type & Size	Total Number

Chemical	Estimated Total Amount

EVIDENCE LOG

Ex. #	Sampled Y/N	Disposed Y/N	Location	Description

Your Initials	**Bottom of Each Page**	Page x of y

Appendix A: Emergency Hotlines

National Response Center	**1-800-424-8800**
(Report major chemical releases; request federal assistance)	
CHEMTREC	**1-800-424-9300**
(Liaison to chemical manufacturers; MSD sheets)	
RCA/Superfund Hotline	**1-800-424-9346**
DOT-Hazmat Information	**1-202-366-4488**
OSHA Hotline	**1-800-321-6742**
NIOSH Information	**1-800-356-4674**

For Product Safety Concerns and Information please contact our
EU representative GPSR@taylorandfrancis.com Taylor & Francis
Verlag GmbH, Kaufingerstraße 24, 80331 München, Germany